100 GREATEST SPORTS HEROES

100 GREATEST SPORTS HEROES

BY MAC DAVIS

ILLUSTRATED BY SAMUEL NISENSON

GROSSET & DUNLAP, INC.

PUBLISHER·NEW YORK

TO THE 100 GREATEST

"There is no greater glory for a man as long as he lives than that which he wins by his own hands and feet."— HOMER, The Odyssey

ACKNOWLEDGMENT

THE AUTHOR and the publisher's wish to extend their thanks to these sports writers whose expert knowledge made it possible to select 100 sports figures who truly represent the greatest heroes of sports. No one man among those listed below can be held responsible for every name in the book, since the final selection represents, of course, a consensus.

AL ABRAMS	Pittsburgh Post Gazette
JAMES B. ANDERSON	Greenville News (S. C.)
SMITH BARRIER	Greensboro News (N. C.)
GEORGE BERTZ	Portland Oregon Journal
FURMAN BISHER	Atlanta Constitution
ROYAL BROUGHAM	Seattle Post-Intellegencer
SI BURICK	Dayton News
ROBERT L. BURNES	St. Louis Globe-Democrat
JIMMY BURNS	Miami Herald
EUGENE JEPSON CADOU, JR.	Indianapolis Star
ALBERT T. CARTWRIGHT	
	Wilmington Journal–Every Evening
JACK CHARVAT	Tulsa Tribune
DEE CHIPMAN	
	Salt Lake City Deseret News-Telegram
AL CLARK	Harrisburg Patriot–Evening News
WILL CLONEY	Boston Post
LOUIS COX	Dallas Times-Herald
JIM DAWSON	Shreveport Times
WILLIAM DIEHL	Norfolk Ledger-Dispatch
GEORGE R. EDMOND	
	St. Paul Dispatch and Pioneer Press
ARNOLD A. FINNEFROCK	
	Jacksonville Florida Times-Union
LEO FISCHER	Chicago American
WIRT GAMMON	Chattanooga Times
EV GARDNER	Washington Daily News
WILTON GARRISON	Charlotte Observer
RICHARD HACKENBERG	Chicago Sun-Times
DICK HERBERT	Raleigh News and Observer
JOE HIRSCH	New York Morning Telegraph
BYRON HOLLINGSWORTH	Tampa Morning Tribune
CHARLES JOHNSON	Minneapolis Star and Tribune
RAYMOND JOHNSON	Nashville Tennessean
KENNETH JONES	Peoria Journal
HARRY KECK	Pittsburgh Sun-Telegraph
CHARLES W. KELLOGG	New Haven Register
DAVE KELLY	Washington Post & Times Herald
WILBUR KINLEY	Tampa Times
JACK LAING	Buffalo Courier-Express
BUD LEAVITT	Bangor News
MICHAEL LEE	Jamaica Long Island Press

WILLIAM LEISER	San Francisco Chronicle
FRANKLIN LEWIS	Cleveland Press
JOSEPH P. LOVAS	Passaic Herald-News
HARRY O. MARTINEZ	New Orleans State
REGIS MCAULEY	Cleveland News
LANSING MCCURLEY	Philadelphia News
ERNEST MEHL	Kansas City Star
A. PAUL MENTON	Baltimore Evening Sun
JOHN MOONEY	Salt Lake City Tribune
WEBSTER J. MORSE	
	Boston Christian Science Monitor
MAX MOSELEY	Montgomery Advertiser
JOHN MURPHY	San Diego Union
JERRY NASON	Boston Globe
ZIPP NEWMAN	Birmingham News
DICK PEEBLES	San Antonio Express
J. E. PENLAND	Columbia State
RODGER H. PIPPEN	
	Baltimore News, Post and Sunday American
EDWIN J. POLLOCK	Philadelphia Bulletin
JACK POWERS	Jersey Journal
LEO RIORDAN	Philadelphia Inquirer
WILLIAM T. RIVES	Dallas News
JAMES ROACH	New York Times
JOHN ROGERS	Memphis Press-Scimitar
FRED RUSSELL	Nashville Banner
H. G. SALSINGER	Detroit News
EDWARD W. SCANNELL	Worcester Gazette
W. F. SHERROD	Fort Worth Press
ARTHUR SIEGEL	Boston Traveler
DENNIS G. SMITHERMAN	Mobile Press
LAWRENCE M. STOLLE	Youngstown Vindicator
CRAIG STOLZE	Sioux Falls Argus-Leader
G. W. TAYLOR	Des Moines Register
W. RUSSELL THOMAS	Trenton Times
DAN WALTON	Tacoma News-Tribune
BRAD WILLSON	Columbus Dispatch
ROBERT L. WILSON	Knoxville News-Sentinel
CHARLES YOUNG	Buffalo Evening News
DICK ZEHMS	Long Beach Press-Telegram
SID ZIFF	Los Angeles Mirror
PAUL B. ZIMMERMAN	Los Angeles Times

CONTENTS

MEET THE IMMORTALS

You are about to meet a hundred remarkable men and women. The highlights in the extraordinary lives of these heroes and heroines are briefly told. I have placed no halos about their heads. Their glory is of their own making.

These titans have been brought together from all the popular sports and in each sport their achievements have written some of the most glorious pages of its history. Many of them were pioneers, creating famous "firsts" that no subsequent achievements could dim. Some were figures of such strong and colorful character that the stamp of their personalities is indelibly impressed on their sports. The great records of others become incredible when we see the heroic struggle against "impossible" odds that brought them to victory.

Every sports fan will find here the stories of most of his heroes. It may occasionally happen, however, that a reader will fail to find one of his personal favorites. There are many great sports figures in addition to the hundred selected here as the greatest of the great, and no

two fans will be in perfect agreement as to who those hundred should be. Our selection, however, represents the consensus of the experts—sports writers from every part of the country who enthusiastically offered their knowledge and opinions. The final responsibility, however, is mine.

To the young sports fan these stories will, I hope, reveal the possibilities of sports glory to which boys and girls may aspire, while to the older reader they offer the companionship of the great personalities who have carved their fame in a field where glory comes only through personal performance.

In this hall of fame you will find the influences and inspiration that make greatness, and the human stories of the heartaches and satisfactions that the athlete knows before he becomes a hero. So let's turn the pages and skip through time. Here they are, each in his place on the world's stage as the curtain goes up on history's 100 greatest of sport.

MAC DAVIS

GROVER CLEVELAND ALEXANDER

Alexander the Great

NOT MANY YEARS have passed since the pitching arm of Grover Cleveland Alexander carved its last entry into the record books, but already his feats have become a legend of baseball. What a pitcher he was in his time! A freckle-faced, happy-go-lucky farm boy from Nebraska when he broke into the big leagues, Ol' Pete, as he came to be known, was picked up by the Philadelphia Phillies for the paltry sum of $750. The first game he pitched brought him face to face with no less a star than the ancient and fabulous Cy Young, winningest pitcher in baseball. Alex beat the veteran 1–0 in a hurling duel that spelled the end to that great immortal's career in baseball. On Alexander's shoulders fell the mantle that Cy Young then and there relinquished. And he wore it with distinction as baseball's greatest pitcher of his time.

In his first major league season, Alex won a mere 28 games, a record that still stands as a 20th-century high for a rookie hurler. In 1915, he pitched the Phils to their first National League pennant, winning 31 games. Without the great Alex, Philadelphia went 35 years before winning another.

Ol' Pete toiled in more games, 696, and won more, 373, than any other pitcher in the history of the National League. He holds more records than any other hurler in the league, numbering among them such marks as most shutouts in a season (16), lowest earned-run average (1.22), most one-hit games pitched in a season (4), and most consecutive shutouts (4).

Although he was baseball's outstanding pitcher for nearly 20 years, Alex is best remembered for having created one of the game's most dramatic moments. It came on a gray, overcast afternoon in the 1926 World Series when, as a fading veteran of 39, Alexander shuffled out to the mound in the seventh inning of the Series' deciding game. The bases were full, the redoubtable Tony Lazzeri was at bat. Ol' Pete, dead-tired after winning the previous day, struck out Lazzeri, saved the game, and brought his St. Louis Cardinals a world's championship. That historic moment is indelibly engraved on a plaque in Baseball's Hall of Fame, a permanent record of an event in sports that will live forever.

Ol' Pete's closing years were a shabby mockery of his glory on the mound. Broke, sick and forgotten, he wandered across the land, finding no peace or contentment anywhere. Once, he even popped up momentarily as the leading side-show attraction of a flea circus. When death came at last to release the tortured soul of Grover Cleveland Alexander, there was left behind only the shining memory of the hero he had once been when he wore a major league uniform. But that memory was more than most men are able to leave behind them.

EDDIE ARCARO
Heady Eddie

WHEN PAPA ARCARO heard that his son, Eddie, was playing hookey from school down in Newport, Kentucky, some two decades ago, he was prepared to take stern action against his errant offspring. Eddie came to the conference with his father wearing a long face. "Look, Pa," he said. "What's the use my going to school with the other kids? I weigh 80 pounds and they won't play with me."

"What do you do when you play hookey?" asked his father.

"I go to the race track," replied Eddie. "A man there lets me gallop horses for him."

"Is that what you want to do—ride horses?"

"I can be a jockey," said Eddie. "If you let me."

Mr. Arcaro gave his reluctant consent and Eddie went to work at the track. A trainer watching him gallop a horse shook his head. "Send him back to school," he said. "He'll never be a rider."

But Eddie flatly refused to give up. He finally got a chance to ride his first horse in a real race. He finished a dead last, after losing his cap and whip, and almost falling off his mount.

But still Eddie Arcaro persisted. He went from one track to another, riding whenever he was allowed to. Then one owner, out of pity, practically adopted the homesick kid with the big nose and let him ride his horses.

There could have been no other reason than pity. Arcaro was an awkward and clumsy apprentice in his first years in the saddle. There was not a single wrong thing he did not do during a race. He got left at the post, ran into traffic jams, got boxed and bumped and roughed to a fare-thee-well. And he never got close to having a winner in the first 100 races he rode.

That was Eddie Arcaro, the apprentice jockey. Had it not been for the fact that some trainers saw something they couldn't quite put their fingers on in this hapless youngster, he would long since have been sent packing.

He was still an apprentice when he startled the racing world by winning 14 races in a single week at Sportsman's Park, Chicago. A big stable offered him a fancy contract to ride high-class thoroughbreds. And Eddie Arcaro began the long career that would see him zoom to the top of the world's jockeys.

One of his outstanding feats was the winning of five Kentucky Derbys, a record. The purses he has won for his various trainers after more than 12,000 rides amount to some $15,000,000. Over a period of 15 years he has earned for himself over $100,000 a year. Eight times he has won over $1,000,000 a year in purses. And he has ridden every great horse in the last twenty years and won every major stake in the United States at one time or another.

The King Who Wore Three Crowns

HENRY ARMSTRONG

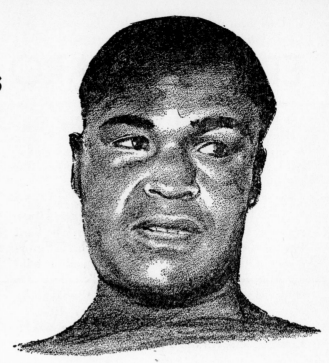

THE BIRTHPLACE of Henry Armstrong was a hovel in a St. Louis slum. There he entered the world in 1912, the thirteenth child in a miserably poor family.

Henry's childhood was short. Before he entered his teens, he was working as a pin boy in a bowling alley. The few pennies he earned meant the difference between eating and starving.

Always hungry, small, thin and restless, young Henry Armstrong soon broke away from family ties. He began to drift around the country, hitch-hiking, walking, riding the rods of freight trains. Once, when he fell asleep while clinging to the "rods" under a train, Henry tumbled from his perch and was almost killed. Another time, a railroad policeman amusing himself took a shot at the frightened youngster and only barely missed.

The lonely boy took to living in hobo jungles and wandering from place to place. Soon his drifting brought him to the Pacific coast. There he became a bootblack. The scramble for shoeshine customers meant a lot of fights for the boy from St. Louis. Every day another big bully challenged him for his right to earn a few coins. The game little Henry licked them all, one after the other, as they came along. In these battles, his scrawny little body grew strong and hard.

One evening, Henry sneaked into a fight arena where a show was going on. There for the first time in his life he saw a real prize fight. He heard the roar of the crowd, and a new thrill of excitement coursed through him. This was what he had been looking for all his life! This was what Henry Armstrong had been made for!

The skinny kid who had been drifting aimlessly from place to place entered the ring. He was just under twenty years of age when he fought his first professional bout. For five years he traveled the highways and byways, taking on all comers. He met them, on the West Coast, in Mexico, New York, London, Paris. Wherever anyone offered the little man a match, there was Henry Armstrong, ready and eager to mix it to a finish.

There was never anyone like Armstrong in the ring. His fighting style can be compared only with a whirlwind. Tireless and reckless, Henry knew only one way to fight: constant attack, always boring in, never letting up. And the wicked power of his two-fisted attack stretched many an opponent on the canvas.

Then Destiny took hold of Henry Armstrong

and set him on the road to his unique record. He began to toll off knockouts with dizzying regularity. Along the way, Henry ticked off 27 KO's in a row. And, on October 29, 1937, the little man from a St. Louis slum knocked out Petey Sarron in six rounds, and took from him the featherweight championship of the world.

Henry reigned supreme among the 125-pounders. He sought new worlds to conquer. And on May 31, 1938, only eight months after winning his first crown, Henry won the welterweight title away from Barney Ross.

Now Henry Armstrong was the proud possessor of two fistic championship titles. The fight fans of the world were at his feet. The little cyclone of the ring had performed an almost incredible feat in holding two world's championships simultaneously. And then the double-champion fought again. On August 17, 1938, he met the lightweight champion of the world, Lou Ambers. And again a title changed hands!

The hammering fists of little Henry Armstrong brought him his third crown—in less than a year!

Now Henry Armstrong stood at the very peak of the fistic world. He was the only man in history ever to hold three world championships at once. Honors poured in on him thick and fast. Every award a boxer could get was his. And finally his name was placed in Boxing's Hall of Fame.

When Henry finally quit the ring, he was acknowledged on all sides to have been one of the greatest fighters, inch for inch, pound for pound, ever to enter the squared circle.

Some years after Henry Armstrong had deserted the ring, once again he amazed the sports world. This former three-way champion was ordained a Baptist minister. For the leather fists he once wore to glory, he substituted a leather-bound Book. His tremendous fighting heart was devoted to fighting evil.

He Broke the Barrier

ROGER BANNISTER

THROUGHOUT HIS BOYHOOD, Roger Bannister thought of nothing but his future as a doctor. And as soon as he began to study medicine, it became apparent to his teachers that he was a born doctor. When he reached the age of 25, he fulfilled his long-cherished ambition to follow his chosen career. But before vanishing completely into the secluded atmosphere that surrounds a man dedicated to the profession of healing, this young Britisher found time to inscribe his name indelibly on the roll of honor in the world of sports. He did this with the most spectacular athletic feat of the 20th century, a fantastic accomplishment that will be told and retold a thousand times down through the years.

Ever since an Englishman named Charles Lawes nearly a hundred years ago ran the classic one-mile distance in the first recorded time of 4 minutes and 56 seconds, the greatest runners in the world have tried to attain the goal that was set up as the shining but ever-elusive objective of all distance runners—the four-minute mile. Only a handful have come close to achieving that aim. The four-minute mile became a sort of myth in sports, a goal that human beings would never reach.

On May 6, 1954, the myth was irretrievably shattered by Roger Bannister, a tall, spare, stooped Englishman with a big-boned, angular face, ruddy complexion, and a cowlick. A startled world cheered when the news hit front pages around the world. Bannister, the obscure

medical student, had leaped out of a life devoted to his profession to become a hero for eternity by running a mile in the magical time of 3 minutes, 59.4 seconds.

What that record means to the sports-loving world is of course perfectly clear. A myth smashed is a new myth made. Now Roger Bannister belongs to the ages alongside the other great immortals of sports. And yet, oddly enough, Roger Bannister, in his own opinion, is a runner of no especially spectacular talent. Nor did he attempt the miracle four-minute mile to gain glory for himself. To him, the historic feat he accomplished was only the end-point of a scientific experiment by which he wished to prove that a man could run faster than was thought possible.

Roger Bannister was born at Harrow, England. His father, a minor Treasury official, cared little for sports. Almost from the time he could walk, Roger's parents had dedicated the boy to a career as a doctor.

Roger was 13 when he won his first race, a three-mile cross-country run. When he entered Oxford, his ambition was to make the college crew. But he soon gave up his hopes. He turned to track, and his deep curiosity about the science and mechanics of running soon conquered his love of rowing.

He was only 17 when he ran his first mile as a freshman at Oxford. He finished far back, and his time was slower than five minutes. A year later, at 18, he won his first race for Oxford in a meet against Cambridge. Again his time was not impressive. Nevertheless, his victory brought from young Bannister a remark which sounded like a boast but was really based on cold scientific fact. The young medical student said that he thought a mile could be run in four minutes. "Who knows?" he added softly. "I might be the one to do it."

Roger Bannister thereupon began his scientific study and rigorous training to reach that objective. By the use of instruments, he calculated to the last decimal point how much oxygen he used for each breath, and how best to expend it. At the same time, while surrounded by charts for guidance, he trained constantly.

No criticism of his novel training methods and scientific research into the mechanics of running turned Bannister from his goal. Even when he was badly beaten in the 1952 Olympics, his failure to prove the value of his training methods did not sway him from his purpose.

Finally, Roger Bannister came to the point where he felt his scientific experiments had been completed. On a dreary, cold, wet and windy day, he went to the Oxford University track to put his theories to the acid test. His parents and a few hundred others were present. The young medical student took the track against three of the fastest milers in England.

The rest is history. Running strictly according to his charts and theories, Roger Bannister ran his miracle mile in 3:59.4, to become the first man in recorded history to speed across this distance in less than four minutes. When he broke the tape at the close of that electrifying race, Roger Bannister became an immortal of sports. Within a few weeks Bannister was joined on the far side of the four-minute mark by John Landy of Australia. And now that the barrier is broken others will run the four-minute mile. But all the glory belongs to Roger Bannister. He broke the barrier.

Slingin' Sam

SAMMY BAUGH

ONE DAY in a long-ago September, the trainer of the Texas Christian University football squad noticed a frail-looking freshman donning a uniform in the dressing room. He turned to the freshman coach with a frown on his face. "You must be out of your mind to let this skinny kid play football," he protested. "Just look at him. You'll be lucky if he survives one scrimmage, much less a whole game."

No trainer could have been more mistaken. The skinny kid, later known to the world of football fans as Sammy Baugh, went on to play freshman, varsity and professional football for twenty years before he was through. In college, Sammy was one of the great stars of the game. In the professional ranks, he set marks that should endure as long as the game itself. For he played fifteen years in the grueling National Football League and remained one of the most scintillating stars while playing longer than any other man in the game.

In all football history, mighty few gridiron greats have lasted as long as Slingin' Sammy Baugh. No one ever had to withstand the pressure and sheer physical beating the great passer underwent over the years. In every game he played, Baugh was a marked man every minute

he was on the field. There was no way to beat the Washington Redskins, the team Sammy played with throughout his pro career, unless he could be stopped. Because of this, Baugh was subjected to a great deal of abuse, legal and illegal, on the gridiron. The tall, slim quarterback had to learn to protect himself under the powerful onslaught of enemy players—and he learned well. Early in his pro career, Sam taught the boys a lesson that was never forgotten.

One afternoon a brutal 240-pounder started a personal feud with the frail-looking Baugh. As Sammy took a pass from center and straightened to pass downfield, the big brute burst through the Redskin line and hammered the Texan to the turf with a thud. That was all right with Sammy because he was accustomed to being banged around a little. But when the giant bully took to applying thumb, fist, knee and elbow to the Baugh anatomy, Sammy felt it was time to put a stop to the proceedings. In the next huddle, Sammy asked his own linemen to let the big fellow crash through unhindered.

Baugh took his usual place in the Redskin backfield and called for the snap from center. As he received the ball, the big brute who had previously mauled Sammy, came crashing through with a howl of triumph and headed straight for the slim, poised Sammy Baugh.

Slingin' Sam just stood where he was in seeming unconcern. To the unsuspecting eye, he was only looking for a receiver downfield. Just as the giant tackler was about to envelop him in his massive clutch, Sammy let fly with all the force of the powerful slingshot arm that had made him the greatest forward passer in all football history.

But the ball did not sail down the field to seek out its waiting receiver. Instead, the pigskin caught the onrushing giant smack between the eyes. The blow knocked him colder than a frozen mackerel. The big guy, with a bump on his forehead as big as a grapefruit, was dragged unconscious from the field. And neither he nor anyone else ever again tried to rough up Sammy Baugh outside the limits of fair play.

As a pro football player, Baugh created over a dozen fantastic passing records. Among them were the top mark for number of passes attempted, 2983, and most passes completed, 1689. His passes have gained a grant total of more than four miles of ground. He completed nearly 60% of his passes, a phenomenal record. He was, as well, one of the finest punters in the game and in the minds of many experts, professional football's finest defensive player.

Six times he led the National Football League in passing, and three times in punting average. And, one year, as if to break the monotony, Sammy led the league in intercepting forward passes thrown by the opposition!

The skinny kid from Texas certainly went a long way in football for a youngster who seemed too frail to play at all. His rubber slingshot arm and his uncanny accuracy brought him not only a comfortable fortune but also immortal fame as the greatest forward passer in the game.

DON BUDGE
Red-headed Comet of the Courts

ALTHOUGH HISTORY and legend may grant to Bill Tilden the honor of being called the greatest tennis player of all time, it was the red-headed, freckle-faced, long-legged Don Budge who successfully brought off the biggest one-man coup in the game of tennis. It was a feat that Tilden himself never accomplished and consisted of winning in one year the four major national singles championships. Budge did just that in 1938 when he scored brilliant victories over the world's best in the United States, British, French and Australian title tournaments.

Curiously enough, J. Donald Budge came to tennis as a youngster with no real love for the game. It took a lot of coaxing by an older brother to get young Don to step on the court. Then, in 1930 when Don was 15, his brother further egged him into entering the California Boys' championship tournament. Don practiced hard for a week before the start of the competition, and then went out and swept the field from his path, winning the crown. It was a perfect score for the youngster—his first tournament, his first championship.

It was then that Don Budge suddenly realized that his racquet could be a key to a lot of doors. He began to play in earnest. At 16 he was playing in senior competition and winning his share of matches. A year later, he came east and won the National Junior championship. Now he was well on his way to the top.

Don, who was not only shy but more than usually clumsy, worked hard at the game he had adopted as his main pursuit. He labored to improve his technique, and his backhand became the most powerful stroke in the game. When he was barely 20, he was a member of the United States Davis Cup team.

It was in 1937 that Don Budge reached his peak. He lost not a single match that year and crowned his achievements by leading the United States team in the recapture of the Davis Cup, coveted symbol of world supremacy. The Cup had been lost in 1926, and when the triumphant Budge brought it back to these shores, he was hailed as a conquering hero.

Already tennis champion of all the world, Budge in 1938 really climbed to a solitary peak on top of all the world of amateur tennis. Monarch of all he could survey, Don turned professional. The year before, an offer to play for pay had been declined by the big redhead, though the $50,000 dangled before him had been a tremendous temptation to a young man who had never had too much money. But in 1938, after helping his country retain the Davis Cup, the grateful officials of amateur tennis gladly blessed his switch from amateur to professional tennis.

Having turned pro at 23, Don soon showed that even in that high-powered field he stood head and shoulders above them all. And he remained a topnotch pro player until he reached the venerable age of 40.

DICK BUTTON
Poetry on Ice

THE FIGURE-SKATING INSTRUCTOR, a wise old professional, took one look at the pudgy little boy standing before him and then turned to the lad's father. "Mr. Button," he said, "I'd advise you to save your money. Never in a million years could your son become a good figure skater. He lacks co-ordination, he's clumsy, and he's too fat. It would be a waste of time for me to try to teach him anything!"

If the story ended there, one of the greatest careers in the history of figure skating would have been lost to the world. But the boy, Dick Button, refused to be turned aside from his ambition. Despite the ridicule and scorn of his friends and playmates, Dick continued to work and practice. And, with his father's encouragement, Dick, in the next few years, carved out the most remarkable record ever made on ice skates.

Dick's determination to make good was handsomely rewarded when he was barely 16 years of age. He won the United States figure-skating championship, to become the youngest to hold the title. After that first victory, one crown after another fell to his flashing skates. And in his 19th year, while still a student at Harvard,

Button was the proud possessor of the five major figure-skating titles: United States, North American, European, Olympic, and World—a breathtaking accomplishment.

Nor was that the limit to Dick's complete mastery of the field of figure skating. Altogether, he won five world titles, seven United States crowns in a row, two Olympic championships and three consecutive North American titles. And all this—every amateur title and championship—came to the handsome young man from Englewood, New Jersey before he had reached his 21st birthday!

To be acclaimed in every corner of the globe as the greatest figure skater in the world is indeed a high achievement—but to reach such heights before the age of 21!

When he reached 21, Dick found that there were no worlds left to conquer in amateur ranks. Every title and every crown was in his possession, or had been. A tempting offer to enter professional figure skating was made to him, and Dick Button, just old enough to sign his own contract, accepted $150,000 to turn pro in an ice show. All the championships in the world, and $150,000—not bad at all for a lad of 21!

WALTER CAMP
Father of Football

WALTER CAMP entered Yale as a student in 1876, only seven years after the first intercollegiate football game had been played. Although he was small by the standards of the day, Camp went out for football and played at halfback for four years.

The game then was nothing like it is today, being a kind of combination of rugby, football and soccer. There were no permanent rules. Some games were played with 25 players on a side, others with 15. Nevertheless, Walter, as a player, came to love football. And when his playing days ended, he remained at Yale as coach of the football team without pay. Blessed with a good imagination, he soon thought up new and revolutionary ideas for the sport. He began to put his ideas into practice.

First of all, he gave the game a complete set of rules. He set the official number of players at eleven men a side, no more, no less. He invented the scrimmage method of putting the ball in play. He developed team signals, used guards as interference on end runs and originated the snapback from center. It was Camp who first instilled into his players the idea: "Watch the ball!" It was also he who introduced the idea of four downs to gain ten yards, which

became the set rule for modern football. The scoring system for touchdowns and field goals is also handed down to us by Camp.

As a champion of the game he loved so fiercely, Camp led the fight to save the game when certain college administration officials frowned on it as a waste of time. The changes he introduced made football less a bloody brawl between two massive groups of giants and more the scientific and skillful exhibition of team coordination it is today.

Camp achieved undying fame when he originated the idea of selecting each year the eleven best players in the nation. He did this in 1889 when he named the first All-America team in intercollegiate football. For 36 years thereafter, Camp chose the dream team of the year and his choice was generally accepted as the only genuine selection. To be named to the Walter Camp All-America came to be the most cherished ambition of every college player in the land.

Football has come a long way since he played, coached, and chose the first All-America, but the fabulously popular game of today owes its origin to Walter Camp, the "father of American football."

ROY CAMPANELLA
The Happy Warrior

ALL THAT Roy Campanella ever wanted in life was to play baseball—not for fame and fortune—just to play ball. No man in the game played it with more gusto, or derived more sheer pleasure out of squatting behind home plate or swinging a bat. But fate had big things in store for the happy backstop of the Brooklyn Dodgers. After only five full seasons in the National League, Campy held most of the records a catcher can have. Twice he had been named the Most Valuable Player in the league. Almost from the first day he drew on his chest protector and mask for the Dodgers, he had been held by most experts to be the best catcher in baseball.

By the time he had completed his fifth full season of major league ball in 1953, Campy had been catching in professional ball for 17 years. He had been a kid of 15 when the Bacharach Giants, a Negro team, got interested in him. The owner of the team approached Roy's mother.

"No," she said. "My boy can't play with you if you have to play Sundays. Sunday is for church-going."

The owner of the Bacharach Giants finally agreed to permit young Roy to go to church Sundays before game-time. And what was more important, he offered to pay Roy's mother $25 every week-end if she let the boy play.

The family was poor, and the offer was too tempting. Roy started catching for the club. Soon he was spotted by the best of the Negro big-time clubs, the Baltimore Elite Giants. Roy signed with them to catch on a monthly salary basis—without informing his mother. When he came home after signing, he was bursting with pride. His mother brushed his words aside. "Where's the $25 you're supposed to bring me, Roy?" she demanded.

When Roy tried to explain that he did not have it but would have lots more at the end of

12

the month, his mother gave him a whipping for throwing away good money.

However, Roy was now well on his way to stardom. In his first season with the Baltimore Elite Giants, the youngster—he was still under 16—caught 150 games and junketed from one end of the country to the other. In later years, it was nothing for the durable backstop to average 250 to 300 games a year, winter and summer, from coast to coast, and from Canada to South America.

So barnstorming with a Negro semi-pro team was no bed of roses for the young catcher. The team went where games could be played, and sometimes Roy was behind the plate in four different games a day. He played in shabby parks, traveled long distances in broken-down buses, caught meals on the run, and pretty poor ones at that. His earnings rarely passed the $100 a month level.

But Roy loved baseball, even when he played a nine-inning game for fifty cents and a couple of dried-out sandwiches. When the Dodgers signed him in 1946, it was just another contract to Roy Campanella. He was sent to Nashua, in the New England League, at a salary of $1,000 for the year, plus a $300 bonus. There he soon showed that he was much too good for the class of ball he was in. The next season or two, Roy moved around through the Dodger farm system. And then, one day in 1948, Branch Rickey, who guided the Brooklyn destinies, called him in.

"Roy," said Rickey, "I know you're the best catcher we have, but I'd like you to go to play in St. Paul."

"If I'm the best, why can't I stay with Brooklyn?" asked the stocky catcher with logic.

"I want you to do it as a favor to me," replied Rickey. "I want to break down the race barriers at St. Paul."

"Why pick on me?" asked Campy, swallowing hard. "I'm no pioneer, I'm a catcher and that's all I want to be. If you send me to St. Paul, that's where I'll go. But I'll go because I'm a ballplayer."

Two weeks later, Roy was back at Brooklyn. The Dodgers had found it impossible to get along without the squat catcher. And no player has more clearly shown his right to be in the big leagues. After three years, he had won the coveted honor of being named Most Valuable Player in the National League for the first time. Two years later, the honor was repeated. Four successive times, he caught the entire game in the All-Star meeting between the two major leagues. His slugging and great backstopping led the Dodgers to National League pennants in 1949, 1952 and 1953. And in 1953, he set new records for catchers by slugging out 41 home runs and driving in 142 runs, while numerous other records fell before the powerful bat of the great Dodger backstop.

At the close of the 1953 baseball season, after only six years in the big leagues, already the fame of Roy Campanella was a growing legend for the story books. For not only was he acclaimed as the finest backstop in the majors, but a catcher worthy to be ranked with the all-time greats of the national pastime. It is possible that before this Happy Warrior is done with major league glory, he will have engraved his name in the Hall of Fame not only as a baseball pioneer—the first Negro catcher in big league history—but also as the first and greatest catcher of them all!

ALEXANDER CARTWRIGHT

Father of Baseball

WHILE THE ORIGINS of baseball are lost in a welter of claims and controversy, one thing is certain. *Modern* baseball, as it is played today, was the offspring of the fertile mind of one of America's earliest players, a man named Alexander Cartwright.

It was in 1845 that the Knickerbocker Baseball Club, first organization of its kind, was formed. Cartwright was one of the stars of that early team. The Knickerbockers did not want to play the haphazard and disorganized kind of baseball then common. They wanted standard, set rules. Cartwright, who was a draftsman and surveyor, was asked to lay out definite rules of play.

What Cartwright did resulted in fixing the game very much in the manner in which it is played today. He laid out the modern diamond with bases 90 feet apart. A team was to consist of nine men, no more no less. He established foul lines, the idea of three outs per side, unalterable batting orders.

The first game played under the new rules took place in Hoboken on June 19, 1846. To make sure the game followed the new rules, Cartwright umpired instead of playing. An odd note of the contest was that Cartwright fined a player named Davis for swearing. And Davis paid up on the spot—six cents.

Baseball was growing slowly under Cartwright's new rules when the gold rush to California began. In March, 1849, Cartwright, an adventurous soul, took off to make his fortune. Traveling overland, he reached Missouri in seven weeks. His diary, which has been preserved, contains this entry:

1849. APRIL 23. *Independence, Mo.* During the past week we have passed the time hunting, fishing and playing baseball. It is comical to see the mountain men and Indians playing the new game. I have the ball with me that we used back home.

So it was that Alexander Cartwright carried with him to the far reaches of the country the game he had standardized in New York. Like Johnny Appleseed before him, Cartwright spread the seeds of baseball across the length and breadth of America.

A few weeks in California was as much as Cartwright wanted of the gold rush. He played a few games of baseball with the prospectors and frontiersmen, and then set sail for home on a vessel bound first for China.

Cartwright fell ill on the ship and was put ashore at Honolulu. While recovering there from his illness, he fell in love with the new country and decided to spend the rest of his life there.

In his new home, Cartwright continued to spread the gospel of modern baseball. When he died in 1892, he had become one of Honolulu's most respected citizens.

Alexander Cartwright was elected to Baseball's Hall of Fame in 1939. The honor is rightfully his, whether the controversy about the beginnings of the game is ever settled or not—for there is no doubt that he is truly the father of modern baseball.

FLORENCE CHADWICK

Queen of the World's Waterways

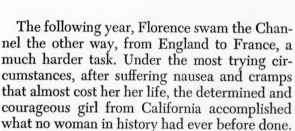

FLORENCE CHADWICK was not quite 13 when she finished second in a backstroke swimming race for the national championship. Hopes were high that the sturdy California girl would some day be a champion. However, she never came any closer to winning a national event than she had in that backstroke race. She could swim at good speed for miles and miles, but she could not confine her talents to a small pool of water. Coaches sadly called the ambitious girl a misfit and washed their hands of her.

But Florence was a determined little girl. If she couldn't sprint short distances, she could train for long ones. Grimly she went on practicing every day in the rough ocean water near her home in San Diego. Always she bore in mind the motto she had pasted into her scrap book: "Winners never quit; quitters never win."

She began to win long distance races. Ten times she won the La Jolla, California, rough-water event against men, seven times the Ocean-side marathon, at least once every other marathon race on the Pacific coast.

She was nearly 30 when she decided to tackle the biggest swimming feat of them all, the English Channel crossing. For years she had been working and saving money for the attempt, and now she felt that she was ready for the toughest swim of her life.

On August 8, 1950, Florence Chadwick slipped into the water and began to swim towards the distant English shore. Only two or three idlers watched the American girl enter the water. In a boat beside her, her father crouched, cheering her on, feeding her from time to time.

13 hours and 20 minutes later, Florence Chadwick emerged from the icy waters and stepped on English soil. She had covered the gruelling 19 miles in time that smashed a 25-year-old record. And she had become famous.

The following year, Florence swam the Channel the other way, from England to France, a much harder task. Under the most trying circumstances, after suffering nausea and cramps that almost cost her her life, the determined and courageous girl from California accomplished what no woman in history had ever before done.

In 1952, she broke another long-standing record when she swam the harsh 24-mile distance from Catalina Island to Los Angeles. A television audience of nearly 50,000,000 this time watched her on their screens with breathless interest as she negotiated the treacherous currents and tides of the Catalina channel in 18 hours.

By now all the world was acknowledging whole-heartedly that Florence Chadwick was the greatest woman swimmer known. But there was more before her. In 1953, she swam the Bosporus from Europe to Asia, and then swam it the other way. Then she conquered the shark-infested Straits of Gibraltar to North Africa. No challenge was too difficult for her to meet. The girl once called a misfit had overcome the most forbidding waters in the world through sheer determination and courage, to become the Queen of the World's Waterways!

The Georgia Peach

TY COBB

TYRUS RAYMOND COBB was a gangling youngster of 17 when he decided that he was going to become a ballplayer. His father, who wanted Ty to be a doctor or a lawyer, did not like the idea. But Ty was not to be turned aside from his ambition. One spring evening in 1904, he sat down and wrote letters to every club in the South Atlantic League, asking for a tryout.

Days passed without an answer. At last, there was a note. The Augusta club was willing to take a look at him. But he would have to pay his own way to the tryout.

When Ty arrived at the ballpark, he was put into center field immediately. He hit a double and a homer in four times up, and scored two runs. But after the next game, he was released because Augusta's regular center fielder had finally reported to the club. Cobb went to Anniston of the Southeastern League. There he did so well that Augusta asked him to come back and play for them again.

In the opening game of the 1905 season, Ty Cobb was back in center field for Augusta. He cost his team a shutout when he started late for a fly ball and missed the catch. The reason for the error was ludicrous. Ty had been eating popcorn instead of paying attention to the game.

So furious with his young outfielder was the Augusta manager that he sold him to another club at once for two dollars cash. But the owner of the Augusta club canceled the sale. Ty rejoined Augusta. And so well did he play that his salary was raised after a few weeks from $90 to $125 a month.

Detroit in 1905 had the right to select one player from the Augusta roster as the result of a deal made earlier between the two clubs. An umpire who had been watching the youngster all season advised the Tigers' owner to take Cobb. And Detroit, although dubious about the quality of the brash young man, finally agreed to take him. The Tigers paid Augusta $700 for the contract of Ty Cobb. Thus began the big-league career of the man many consider base-

16

ball's greatest player, the fabulous "Georgia Peach."

Nothing can tell more about the kind of player Ty Cobb was than the list of records he made. Ty played major league ball for 24 years. He engaged in most games, 3,033; was at bat most times, 11,429; scored most runs, 2,244; made most hits, 4,191; stole the most bases, 892; and stole a record 96 bases in one season.

Ty Cobb holds the highest lifetime batting average, a mark of .367. He was batting champion in the league 12 times, 9 of them in succession. He batted over .300 twenty-three different times, missing the charmed figure only in his rookie year in the majors. He made more than 200 hits in nine different seasons. He is co-holder of the record for the highest seasonal batting average, .420, and batted over .400 three times. One last record: on May 5, 1925, Ty Cobb set a mark for most total bases in a game when he whacked out two singles, a double and three home runs in a single game, a total of 16 bases.

The figures are fantastic, but they are cold. They do not describe the dynamic, pugnacious, arrogant, conceited, hot-tempered Ty Cobb. He was the most cordially hated man in the game. Even his own teammates fought with Ty, and some of the battles in which the fiery Georgia Peach engaged have become historic. On the field or off, Ty gave or sought no quarter. He would fight anyone any time, and the infielder who dared to block a basepath when Ty was coming down the line did so at risk to life and limb.

But as a player, Ty Cobb was superb. Combining strategy, speed and a fiery competitive spirit, he blazed his way through all opposition, forcing all baseball to give him respect and admiration, if not affection.

Even in his last year as a player, the worn-out 42-year-old Cobb batted .323. His salary had risen with the years and he had invested it wisely. When he quit baseball, Cobb was well on his way to wealth. Before long, he had become a millionaire several times over.

To honor his parents, the Georgia Peach made a grant of $100,000 to start the Cobb Hospital in his native state. Then he established a foundation at the University of Georgia to help needy students complete their education.

Today, Ty Cobb is just a legend in baseball, along with all the other great stars of yesterday. But the fiery immortal who once was sold for a couple of dollars has richly endowed the game he loved with a record of accomplishment that will shine as long as baseball is played anywhere in the world.

EDDIE COLLINS

Sharpest Second-sacker

IT WAS IN 1906 that Edward T. Collins left college to make his debut with the Philadelphia Athletics as a big-league ballplayer. Nervous and jumpy, and with a fiery temper and burning eagerness to try anything, Collins impressed most baseball men who looked him over as unlikely to last very long in the majors. However, Eddie almost immediately went to the top as baseball's finest second baseman. It was due to his inspired play and fiery leadership that the Athletics won four pennants in five years. And later it was the same Collins who drove the Chicago White Sox to two flags in three years. With Eddie Collins as their second baseman, these were the two most accomplished clubs of their time.

Making good as a player when so many thought he would quickly burn himself out was not all that Eddie Collins accomplished. No other man in major league history lasted as long as he in big time play. Eddie Collins was an active major league star for 25 long hard years.

In his quarter-century of active duty in the national pastime, Collins created many records. Baseball's greatest second baseman amassed a lifetime batting average of .333. His lightning speed on the basepaths, his quick mind, and his uncanny knack of knowing when to go, brought him the tremendous total of 744 stolen bases over the years. At times, his feats were almost fantastic. On September 11, 1912, in a game against the Detroit Tigers, he stole six bases, a record. And then, to make that feat even more impressive, he duplicated it eleven days later against the St. Louis Browns.

No man was more skillful at the keystone sack than Eddie Collins, and he led the league in fielding percentage year after year. It is good to note that Eddie was so gentlemanly a player that he was ejected from a game not more than six times in all the 25 years he played.

Although Eddie Collins was one of the greatest of our baseball players, he is, oddly enough, remembered more for a peculiar incident that occurred during a World Series than he is for his all-round accomplishments. The incident took place during the 1917 Series. Collins was on third when a rundown play saw him caught between third and home. In the jockeying back and forth that followed, Heinie Zimmerman, the New York Giant third baseman, chased the elusive Collins from third base all the way to home plate—with the run that won the contest and the World Series!

The fact that in that same Series, Eddie Collins batted .409 to lead all the players, and that he played for 25 years and then coached and managed for 15 more, are forgotten. It is ironic that so great a player and inspirational leader should be best remembered as the man who won a foot race with a third baseman!

HIRAM CONNIBEAR

The Connibear Stroke

AROUND THE TURN of the last century, a gaunt, lean man by the name of Hiram Connibear was a trainer with the Chicago White Sox. In 1906, after the legendary "Hitless Wonders" had won the World Series, he asked for a $200 raise for the next season. It was refused. In a huff, Connibear took a job to train the football squad at the University of Washington.

At the university, the students resented Connibear's roughness and uncouth dugout expressions. It seemed likely that he would soon be fired again. But Connibear got word that the school was thinking of organizing a crew and was seeking a rowing coach. He volunteered for the job—and offered to do it without pay so long as he was retained as football trainer.

Reluctantly, the Washington authorities appointed Connibear coach of crew. They did so without knowing one important thing: that Connibear hated water, that he couldn't swim, and that he had never in his life even seen a rowing shell.

But if Connibear was ignorant of rowing, he was no fool. The muscle-slapper bought a few books on the subject and began to study the sport. Late at night, he would sneak down to the boathouse with his books and practice the rowing strokes. He tried to figure out what made an eight-oared racing shell run through the water, what was the best and smoothest stroke for the men, how they should use their arms, legs, backs.

Meanwhile, discontent spread on the campus. Word had leaked out that the new coach knew absolutely nothing about crew racing. A mutiny was in the air when finally Connibear decided to take the bull by the horns. He called together the entire rowing squad and locked himself into the boat-house with them away from all prying eyes. Then he proceeded to give them a talk. In his rough and uneducated way, he told them how ignorant he was about his duties as crew coach, how he had been studying to dope out the best possible type of stroke for them. The boys listened in fascinated silence. In the sudden hush, Connibear began to weep.

"Boys," he said, "I beg you, wait a little. I'm on the road to something worth while. I'll make a great crew out of you—if you give me the chance!"

Connibear went out and left the boys to make up their minds what to do. After a few minutes of discussion, they all decided to stick by him.

A little later, Connibear finally discovered how to make a racing shell go faster than it ever had gone before. Using revolutionary principles of engineering, the unknown coach evolved a rowing stroke that turned the whole sport upside down. With the new Connibear stroke, Washington crews from that moment became the mightiest in the land. What is more, Washington became the source of practically every coach in collegiate rowing. Down through the years, the greatest college crews have used the Connibear stroke.

Connibear died years ago in a fall from a tree where he had climbed to watch a crew race, but the master stroke he discovered lives on. As long as college crews go down their watery ways in skimming shells, just so long will Hiram Connibear be remembered as the man who completely revolutionized the ancient sport of rowing to become one of the greatest coaches in rowing history.

JAMES B. CONNOLLY

First American Olympic Champion

JAMES B. CONNOLLY was a freshman at Harvard when it was announced that, after 1500 years, the Olympic games were going to be revived at the site of ancient Athens in Greece. Connolly was a nobody as far as sport fame can be measured. All he could boast of was an otherwise normal uncle who had flabbergasted a lot of people by jumping in and out of 27 mackerel barrels in rapid succession. Odd as that feat was, it had been enough to interest the young Connolly to try jumping himself— but he stuck to a more respectable sport, the hop, step and jump. And when he heard that the Olympic games were going to be revived, he decided to try to enter his favorite event.

He sought permission from his college authorities to leave for Greece to seek Olympic glory. But the Harvard officials thought Connolly's idea was foolhardy and refused. So Connolly just walked out of school and, at his own expense, set out for his goal. All he could afford

was a cramped and smelly cattle boat. But it was enough, for it would get him where he wanted to go.

When he arrived at Athens, he learned that he had no time to prepare himself for the hop, step and jump event. It was nobody's fault. The Greek calendar, under which the games were to be run, was 12 days different from the American one.

On his first day in Athens, Connolly was finishing a leisurely breakfast at his modest hotel when an official of the games came hurrying to him to say that the hop, step and jump would be the first event of the Olympics—and that it would take place at two o'clock that very day! The young American was shocked—but at two o'clock he was at the stadium, ready to make his all-out effort for his country.

Competing against the best in the world, before 80,000 fascinated spectators, James B. Connolly hopped, stepped and jumped to victory! It was a great moment in Olympic history, but a greater one in American history. For this made the American flag the first to be hoisted as a sign of victory in the Olympic games! And it was to James B. Connolly, a Harvard freshman who had paid his own way to participate for his country, that the honor went of being the first winner in the modern Olympics.

Connolly never returned to Harvard as a student after making his historic appearance at the Athens festival. Many years later—when the Stars and Stripes had become a very familiar sight atop the victory staff at Olympic games— Connolly did go back to his old school. He returned to lecture—but not, oddly enough, on athletics. For Connolly had become a famous author of sea tales in the years that had passed since 1896. And he returned to Cambridge to lecture not on sports—but on literature!

MAUREEN CONNOLLY
Mighty Little Mo

UNTIL she was ten years old, all that Maureen Connolly was interested in was riding a horse. She might have gone far as an expert equestrienne except for the fact that her family decided to move. The move, as fate would have it, brought the Connolly family just around the corner from the municipal tennis courts in San Diego, California.

One day, the ten-year-old Maureen happened to wander by the courts when the tennis pro was giving a young lady a lesson. He noticed the little girl with her nose against the wire fence and asked her to come inside and bat the ball back to his pupil. Maureen nodded assent and came on the court. And one of the most sensational careers in tennis began at that moment.

The tennis pro took one look at the chunky little girl's form as she swatted a tennis ball— then took another and more startled look. He was amazed that this child who had never in her life held a tennis racquet in her hand should have so beautiful and natural a swing, such fine coordination and power. He offered to give her lessons—and she agreed.

From then on it was all tennis for Maureen Connolly. Within three months, she was able to go as far as the final round in a tournament. Then illness for a while threatened to bring her budding career to an abrupt halt, but she fought it off successfully. Soon she was back on the courts again, and this time she caught the eye of one of California's most famous coaches and teachers of tennis. And little Mo began to apply herself seriously and with burning devotion to tennis.

At 14, Maureen, playing on grass for the first time, won the National Girls' Tournament, to become the youngest winner. Later that year she entered the Nationals at Forest Hills just for the experience. The next year, at only 15, she was ranked tenth among all women in tennis! "Mighty Little Mo" the sports world nicknamed her.

The cool, businesslike demon of the tennis courts finally reached the goal of her young life when she won the National Women's title at Forest Hills in 1951. She was then less than 17 years of age, the youngest tennis champ in history! She repeated her triumph in 1952 and again in 1953, making her at 19 a three-time women's national champion. And each of those years she was voted the Woman Athlete of the Year over the greatest female athletes in all sports.

It was in 1953 that Maureen Connolly became the only woman tennis player in history to win in a single year all the four major tennis tournaments of the world. They included the United States singles title, the Wimbledon crown in England, the Australian tennis championship, and the French women's national tournament.

The unspoiled and self-possessed girl from San Diego with the exploding forehand has gone far in the world of tennis, and the end is far from foreseeable. It is certain, however, that her tennis feats all over the world have earned her a ranking alongside the great stars of the past whose every record she threatens to shatter in the coming years.

21

Magician of the Court

BOB COUSY

Son of a mechanic, Bob had few advantages as a youngster. But he came a long way. Pro basketball has been kind to Bob Cousy. At last report, he was one of the highest-paid in the game, and his income from all sources assures him of the kind of comfort and ease he never had known in his youth.

Oddly enough, it was almost by accident that Bob Cousy became a professional at all. In his last season at Holy Cross, he had set an all-time mark for that school by scoring 582 points. But Bob was only 6 feet tall, and was considered too small for pro play. The demand was for skyscrapers of 6 feet 6 and up.

And there was further worry about his temperament which was deemed to be somewhat withdrawn and taciturn, making it difficult for him to get along with others. Worst of all, Bob Cousy was too fancy on the basketball court, too unpredictable a passer. His deception was so perfect that even his fellow-players for years at Holy Cross were never able to tell when Bob was going to pass to them, or if he was going to pass at all.

It was Boston that got Cousy by drawing his name out of a hat. It happened that there were three college stars up for grabs by the pros in 1950, an Cousy was one of them. Not one of the teams wanted him, but they did want the other two men available. When they couldn't agree on who was to get whom, all three names were put in a hat. Boston drew Cousy—and was stuck with him. Today, the Boston owner wouldn't give up Bob Cousy for half-a-dozen seven-footers plus the United States Mint.

It is almost impossible to describe what Cousy can do with a basketball and even less possible to make it believable. One of the top pro coaches remarked of him, "Nobody believes what they hear of him—till they see him. The fact is that Bob Cousy can do more things with a basketball than any man who ever lived and played."

BOB COUSY was a 16-year-old junior in high school at St. Albans, New York, when he stopped curiously to watch the school team practice basketball one afternoon. He himself had never played the game. The skinny, black-haired kid fell in love with it on the spot. Within a week, he was a full-fledged member of the team. By the end of the 1953–4 professional basketball season, Bob Cousy was acknowledged to be the greatest player in the game, bar none.

Once he made the team, Bob Cousy attacked his new interest with a single-mindedness and devotion that never slackened. From the time he first began to play, he never let up. In high school, he played the full season, then continued all summer at various vacation resorts. In college at Holy Cross where he first attracted national attention, he also played summer, spring and fall, as well as all of the regular season. And even as a professional with the Boston Celtics, Bob played all summer for his own amusement, as well as running a school for young players. In other words, he lived, ate, breathed basketball 12 months of the year and never, even after becoming the greatest in pro ranks, lost his zest for the game.

GLENN CUNNINGHAM

The Miraculous Miler

IT WAS IN THE 1930's that the world first began to hear about a young man from Kansas who was burning up the cinder paths at the classic distance of one mile. And before his running days were over, Glenn Cunningham, the Kansas Flyer, had set a record for courage, and consistent high speed for all the world to shoot at.

Glenn was a schoolboy in his native Kansas when tragedy struck that threatened to ruin his life. He was trapped in a schoolhouse fire. Before he could be rescued from the blazing inferno, Glenn was badly burned. And, what was worst of all for an active boy, it was his legs that were most severely injured.

For almost a year, Glenn was in bed. For a time, even his life was despaired of. When at last the boy's burns had healed, the doctors felt that he would never walk.

But time passed, and a boy with courage fooled the doctors who had expected the worst. For many months, all Glenn could do was limp painfully around his father's farm. Little by little, strength came back to his scarred legs.

He learned to walk again. And then he found he could run. And run he did with the enthusiasm possible only in a boy who had thought he might never even walk.

The burns that Glenn Cunningham had suffered in the schoolhouse fire had not healed without leaving their ugly mark. Where the flesh had been eaten away, thick scar tissue had formed. Because of this, Glenn could not limber up before a race as most runners did. It was necessary for him to prance and contort himself for a long time before he could run freely. To the spectators in the stands, it looked as if the Kansan was showing off on the track below them. And they jeered him thoughtlessly.

Cunningham took the derision in stride. All he was concerned with was getting himself into the best possible condition for the race he was going to run. And when the blood began to course through the scar tissue in his legs, and the pain eased and he felt ready, Glenn Cunningham went out and ran.

In spite of his physical handicap, in spite of the hostility from the stands, Glenn Cunningham became the most consistent mile champion in history. World records fell at his flying heels and national championships by the score. Outdoors, he ran the mile in 4:06.7. Indoors, he sped the distance in the sparkling time of 4:04.4.

But it was his consistency at the distance that made Glenn Cunningham the outstanding runner he was. For the Kansas Flyer ran the mile under 4:10 a total of 20 times! No other runner at the distance has ever approached his record in this respect. And it was all done by a man whose legs were so badly burned and so covered with scar tissue that it was a miracle he could run at all—proof, if any is needed, that a courageous heart can overcome the most discouraging handicap!

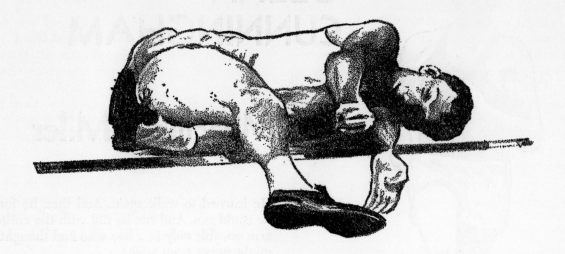

WALT DAVIS
The Kangaroo Kid

IT IS ONE of the paradoxes of life that greatness is more likely to come out of adversity than from an easy existence. Many athletes overcame disabilities to become world champions but no man in history ever leaped higher to achieve such glory than Walt Davis.

It was a wonder that he became an athlete at all for at the age of eight, he was stricken with infantile paralysis. It left him with both legs and one arm paralyzed. He spent weeks in a Beaumont, Texas, hospital and months at home in bed. At nine, Walt had to learn how to walk holding on to the bed. To his parents, it was enough that their son's life had been spared even if his future looked limited. But to the boy himself, a life of immobility was not enough to satisfy him. He did constant exercise, underwent painful massage, and he spent hours daily pumping a bicycle to strengthen his legs. Miraculously, his crippled legs and arm began to come back to life, although, until he was seventeen, he couldn't sit down comfortably, and he couldn't run across an athletic field without stumbling for blood drained from his heels so badly that he had to walk and run on tiptoe until the circulation was restored.

However, despite his handicap, Walt became a star high school athlete in Nederland, Texas. He won four letters for basketball and one baseball letter as a first baseman. By the time he showed up at Texas A & M, Walt Davis had grown into a 200-pound giant towering 6 feet, 8½ inches in height. He was the tallest athlete ever to play basketball for Texas A & M, and he brought that college more publicity than any athlete in its history.

Walt Davis, the star basketball player, became a world famous high jumper in a curious way. For it wasn't until he had entered college that he first started to high jump. He only turned to that sport to escape the drudgery of basketball practice. Texas A & M went in for a heavy schedule of spring basketball practice. Even in spring, it gets plenty hot at College Station, Texas. So, to avoid indoor basketball practice and to escape outdoors where the temperature was more tolerable, Walt went out for the track team. He made it as a high jumper.

He learned fast. By 1952, Walt Davis was the best high jumper in America. He was chosen for the Olympic team that sailed to Helsinki, Finland, for the 1952 Olympic Games. There,

24

Walt Davis won international fame when he made a record leap of 6 feet 8¼ inches to win the high jump crown. He was the first American gold medal winner of the 1952 Olympic Games.

However, upon his return to the United States, Davis was not satisfied to bask in the glory of being a record-holding Olympic champion. There was still one high jump mark he had not reached, and he was determined to overtake it. It was the world's record of 6 feet, 11 inches, which had been set for this event in 1941. So, Davis began to plan how to achieve his goal to become the high jump champion of history.

An unusual idea struck him and he put it into immediate action. He began to take ballet lessons to improve his form so that he could leap higher than any man ever had in history. He worked hard and long at the intricate ballet

figures. Then he entered a track meet for the supreme test. And he almost broke his leg instead of the record he wanted.

But Walt Davis persisted in his chosen task. The historic moment came at last at the A.A.U. Track and Field Championships at Dayton, Ohio in 1953. On his first two attempts to break the world's record, Walt Davis failed. But on his third and last try, he soared higher than any man in history, leaping over the high-jump bar at the incredible height of 6 feet, 11½ inches!

At 22, this amazing man who had won universal fame by leaping higher than any other human in history, deserted the sport in which he was king of all he surveyed, and became a professional basketball player with the Philadelphia Warriors.

NED DAY
Gentleman Bowler

AS A HIGH SCHOOL STUDENT in West Allis, Wisconsin, Ned Day was a fine athlete, winning letters for football, swimming and track. He might have gone on to become a college star in those sports, for he was offered a scholarship by the University of Wisconsin. But Ned Day decided that his future lay along a different path. In pursuing that path, he became the world's greatest bowler.

One day, while still at high school, 15-year-old Ned wandered into a bowling alley, curious to see what went on inside. As luck would have it, Harry Ganzel, a world-famous bowler and owner of the alleys, was playing, and Ned stopped to watch him roll a perfect 300-game. The cheers that went up from the spectators at Ganzel's feat excited Ned Day. And he made up his mind on the spot to become a bowler.

The next day, Ned went back to the bowling alleys to learn how to play. Under Ganzel's watchful eye, the slim youngster bowled a miserable 63. It was a very modest beginning indeed. But Ned Day went on from there. And he did not stop until he reached the very top in the world of bowling.

Before he was 35, Ned Day had won the world's match championship five times, a record that has never been approached by anyone. Among his victims, he included practically every player of quality in the world. For those still reluctant to take him on, Ned Day posted cheerfully a $5,000 check to bind a match for that sum against any challenger. There were no takers, proving, if further proof were needed, that Day was bowling's greatest.

Ned did not climb to the top in a hurry. It took the young bowler many hard hours and months of constant practice. But Ned Day was always filled with supreme confidence that he would at last be the best in his chosen field of sport. He developed skill to a high degree and a style of his own that approached perfection of form. And, as soon as he was capable of it, he began to enter the big tournaments. Soon he was a man to reckon with. He finished fourth in his first national meet, hitting the headlines with one perfect game of 300. Over a ten-year period, he averaged 202 in American Bowling Congress meets. He set a world's record of 1,393 pins for five games and 2,671 for ten games.

He was the first bowler ever to hold three match titles at the same time. He won the individual, shared the doubles and five-man team titles. All in all, Ned Day rolled 27 perfect games and was twice chosen Bowler of the Year.

The game brought Day a fortune and silenced his earlier regrets that he had not become an engineer or a big businessman, as he could have. His income from bowling soared to many thousands a year, coming from his efforts as a teacher, competitor and demonstrator. Slim, dapper, beautifully dressed, Ned Day came to be known as the gentleman bowler. And, if added to that, it is noted that he was not only a gracious winner but a graceful loser the few times he got licked, it is fair to say that Ned Day, bowling's biggest money winner and greatest match player, has earned his right to be included among the immortals of sports.

CLARENCE DeMAR

The Shuffler

CLARENCE DeMAR, one of the truly great marathon runners of modern times, and the most amazing of all time, was born on an Ohio farm. As a boy, Clarence suffered from a physical handicap, one that he had from birth. To overcome it, he took up running as an exercise.

One day, a friend who was watching Clarence shuffling through his painful running exercises suggested as a joke that he enter a long-distance race. DeMar accepted the challenge and sent in his name. The race, over a distance of ten miles, was a handicap affair. And the unknown Clarence DeMar received a generous handicap at the start.

To everyone's amazement, his own not excepted, the Ohio farm boy won the race. His friend apologized for having laughed at him. But DeMar, now flushed with victory, began to think seriously of taking up long-distance running as a career, in spite of his handicap. He decided to enter the annual Boston Marathon, famous race at the distance of 26 miles and 385 yards.

Again Clarence DeMar surprised everyone. Running a strong race, the green and inexperienced youngster finished in second place in that gruelling race against some of the greatest distance runners in the world.

In the years that followed, DeMar ran again and again in the Boston Marathon. Over a stretch of 25 years—a quarter of a century—he never finished worse than third. And, in those same 25 years, he won the Boston Marathon 7 times! At other times, DeMar ran in and won every important marathon race in the world.

When he was 61 years of age, Clarence DeMar, a grizzled veteran of a hundred marathon races, ran at Boston for the 29th time. In spite of his age, and against 141 top runners of the world, DeMar not only managed to complete the long 26-mile-plus grind of the Boston Marathon but also succeeded in finishing well up with the leaders—a remarkable achievement for an old man of 61! When deep in his sixties, he was still running in the annual Boston Marathon, and finishing this gruelling grind to receive a greater ovation than the winner of the race.

But the true measure of Clarence DeMar's greatness was not that he kept running long after most men have given up much quieter pursuits, nor is it even the record he piled up over the years in marathon running. The heroic thing about Clarence DeMar is that he ever ran at all. The handicap with which he was born and that was never cured was a crooked foot!

JACK DEMPSEY

The Manassa Mauler

Although he never smoked nor drank, it was around the taverns of the western towns that Jack found the matches by which he could earn enough to eat. One day, he wandered into such a place. A gang of toughs thought the ragged hobo an amusing spectacle and began to jeer at him. In a moment, a brawl was under way as Jack pitched into all six of his tormentors.

There was one man in that tavern who watched with special interest as the savage young hobo lowered the boom on the toughs. When peace was restored, he talked to him. They came to an agreement. And the stranger—Jack Kearns—became Jack Dempsey's manager.

Jack's manager found that his new charge was right-hand crazy. He tried to make Jack stop throwing it all the time. At last he decided on desperate measures. He bound Jack's right arm to his side and made him box with only the left. And the trick worked. It was that left hand, the famous left hook, which Jack Dempsey was to use to pulverize his opponents and lure into the arenas millions of fans and over $9,000,000 in gate receipts.

With Kearns managing him, Dempsey's career began in earnest. Only two years after they first met, Dempsey went to Toledo to fight a mountain of man named Jess Willard, heavyweight champion of the world. The savage, murderous-punching Dempsey smashed the big lumbering champion to a bloody hulk in three rounds. Dempsey, former hobo and wanderer, was the new heavyweight champion of the world!

PART CHOCTAW INDIAN, part Irish and Scotch, Jack Dempsey as a kid was a wandering hobo. The ragged and unkempt youngster was grateful for a chance to fight in the ring for whatever anyone was willing to pay. Sometimes it was only for a bowl of soup. If he was lucky, a bout might bring him a square meal and clean bed for a night. He knew no home to call his own, no place to lay his head.

For a time he might work as a coal heaver. A few weeks of that, and he would be hopping freights again. Whatever it was, anyone could make him stop immediately by offering him a fight. And he fought everyone—in the ring or out. In the hobo jungles he battled them all, and always hammered his way to victory.

Another day came. Jack went to the small town of Shelby, Montana, to defend his title against Tommy Gibbons. Out of pride and eagerness for publicity, the small town had agreed to pay the champ the sum of $300,000 to appear there in defense of his title. And when Jack left Shelby, he left behind an empty shell, a town that was bankrupt.

Greater and greater grew the crowds that came to watch the great champion fight. When he met the handsome Frenchman, Georges Carpentier, 80,000 paid nearly $2,000,000 to see the fight. Ring history was made that night, for it was the first million-dollar gate in history—and the first time a championship fight had been aired over radio.

Then Dempsey met the big Argentine, Luis Firpo. This time, there were 85,000 screaming fans on hand. Again the gate passed the magic million mark. Six minutes the bout lasted, six minutes of the most dramatic and thrilling action in the ring. Dempsey won with a typical mauling attack.

And then he lost his title, in a match that dumbfounded the fight fans of the nation. For Jack Dempsey had come to be a god in the eyes of fight-followers everywhere, an invincible titan of the ring. But the boxing skill of Gene Tunney outpointed him.

Jack, the fallen hero, tried to come back. This time there were well over 100,000 on hand to see the Manassa Mauler work a miracle. But the clever and cunning new champion held him off. And again Dempsey was beaten. Nevertheless, in losing, he left behind the biggest controversy in ring history. For he had knocked Tunney down for that famous long count—the count that many claimed had taken 14 seconds.

Oddly enough, Jack Dempsey became even more popular as an ex-champion than he had ever been as the king of his division. He was in constant demand all over the world to referee boxing and wrestling matches. His fees were fantastic, ranging as high as the $10,000 paid him in Manila. All in all, Jack managed to earn nearly $10,000,000 in and out of the ring.

And he was generous. With his own unhappy youth ever in his mind, the former hobo from Manassa, Colorado, gave generously of his time and money to worthy causes and deserving charities. He was always on call, for benefits or appearances at hospitals and camps, wherever they wanted to take a look at the fabulous ex-champion.

In all the world there is no better known figure in boxing than the great old champion, Jack Dempsey. To be a millionaire must be a welcome change from the days when he wandered, ragged and alone, in the hobo jungles of the west. But richer by far is the old Manassa Mauler in the love and affection which all the world holds for him, one of the most popular champions in history.

BABE DIDRIKSON

Marvelous Mildred

A TEXAS INSURANCE MAN, whose hobby was his women employees' basketball team, happened to be out scouting for new players one day when he entered a high school gymnasium to watch a game. What he saw made him rub his eyes with disbelief. On the court below him was a girl. About 16, she was strong, firm and graceful. But it was what she was doing with a basketball that astonished him. From all angles, and with uncanny accuracy, the girl was dropping baskets through the cords one after the other, as fast as she could get her hands on the ball.

That was Mildred Didrikson, making her first impact on the world of sports. As soon as the game ended, the Texas insurance man was after her. He persuaded her to move to Dallas, take a job with his company, and play on its girls' basketball team.

By the end of her first season of basketball in Dallas, Babe Didrikson made the woman's All-American basketball team.

Someone then asked Babe whether she would like to try her hand at track and field activities. She had never before been on a cinder path. She began to practice for several events and then, in 1930, entered the National A.A.U. women's track and field championships.

The self-taught girl not only won the broad jump but she broke the world's record for the event. Later the same year, she established new American marks in the javelin throw, the shotput, the baseball throw and the high jump. Then she tried the sprints and hurdles, again breaking records right and left, no matter what the event.

Babe, of course, was an outstanding entrant when the tryouts for the women's Olympic squad came along in 1932. The amazing athlete competed in six races in succession, then in all her field events. Out of eight events, she took six firsts and a fourth.

At the Olympic Games themselves, Babe qualified easily for five events in women's track and field. However, she was permitted to compete in only three of them. She not only won them all, but set a new world's record in each!

The National women's track and field championships of 1932 saw Babe reach the high point of her running and jumping career. Scoring 30 points, the fantastic girl from Texas actually won the meet by herself, with the famous

22-girl squad from the Illinois Athletic Club in second place behind her.

Babe Didrikson's fame as a basketball player and a track and field star should not be allowed to obscure her expertness in a host of other sports. She excelled as a cyclist, a fancy figure skater, a diver and swimmer, a tennis player, a marksman. She was so good a baseball player that she was able to play alongside men professionals and hold her own with them. She could box, play billiards, even football with the men. In fact, there was no sport to which the Babe turned that she could not do well in.

After her all-conquering year of 1932, Babe began to look for new worlds to play in. She decided that golf offered the best possibilities for the future. She had never tried the game before.

In 1934, she entered her first golf tournament. She won it. From that beginning at a new game, Babe went on to prove she was the best woman in the world at the game. Playing with drive and boldness, like a man rather than a woman, Babe smashed every woman's record as she toured the courses. At one time, she ran up a streak of 20 consecutive tournament victories, as phenomenal a string as was ever put together by any golfer. She became the first American girl to win the Women's British Amateur. In 1946, she turned pro, and from that time, earned about a quarter-of-a-million dollars annually.

After having dominated the women's golf world for years, Babe Didrikson, now married to wrestler George Zaharias, was suddenly stricken by what everyone thought was going to be a fatal illness. She was at the very top of her game when she had to leave the golf courses for major surgery. A world of sports fans prayed for her recovery. Gamely she came back to golf like a true champion and again fought her way to the top among the finest female golfers in the world.

No one more richly deserved the honor which the historians of sports bestowed upon her and which the world accepted as a fact—the greatest woman athlete of the 20th century.

Old Bones

HARRISON DILLARD

SINCE THEIR BEGINNING, each playing of the Olympic Games has handed down to posterity one unforgettable sports story. The Games of 1948 will forever be remembered for the triumph of Harrison Dillard, a story to be told and retold in the years to come as the tale of the vindication of Old Bones.

The dream of Olympic victory began to blossom in the heart of Harrison when he was still a frail, scrawny and unknown youngster of 12. An unhappy child of poverty, there was little that the undernourished Negro boy could have except dreams. Jesse Owens had returned from the 1936 Olympics as the greatest sports hero in the world, winner of three major Olympic titles. And 12-year-old Harrison adopted the mighty Owens as his idol. He wanted, beyond all else, to become a sprinter just like him. And, on the wings of his dream, young Dillard reported to the track team at Kennard Junior High School in Cleveland.

His schoolmates took one look at young Harrison and burst out laughing at his skinny body. "Look at him," they yelled. "Look at the sack of bones. Hey, Bones!"

And the school track coach shook his head over Harrison's pipestem arms and legs. "Forget it, kid," he said. "You're not strong enough to run the sprints." Then he relented a little as he saw the boy droop with disappointment. "Go on and see what you can do in the hurdles," he added more kindly. "Maybe you can do better there." So Dillard became a hurdler.

As the years went by, the boy grew bigger and stronger. By the time he enrolled at Baldwin-Wallace College, he was a full-grown track man—and he was still a hurdler.

Harrison Dillard became a celebrated sports hero as a hurdler, the greatest in America, perhaps in all the world. Before the 1948 Olympic Games rolled around, he had compiled an astounding winning streak of 82 consecutive victories. It was a foregone conclusion that Old Bones, world's greatest hurdler, would go to the Games in London and win the Olympic crown he had so long dreamed of winning.

But fate decided to play a cruel joke on him. For when the Olympic tryouts took place, Dillard had a miserable day and failed in his specialty. It was a hard blow to his pride, a heartbreaking setback for the famous track star with an Olympic dream gnawing at his vitals.

But fate couldn't destroy Old Bones. By superhuman effort, he just managed to squeeze himself on to the American team—as a sprinter.

The sports world found it highly amusing that the world's greatest hurdler was going to the Olympics as a runner. The wiseacres said that he was just going along for the boat ride to London. For how could he ever hope to beat the illustrious Mel Patton, world's record holder for the 100, or Barney Ewell who had beaten Patton in the Olympic tryouts? Poor Harrison seemed doomed to Olympic failure from the start.

Then came the big day, the day of the Olympic sprints. Before a wild screaming mob of 83,000 people gathered from all the corners of the world, Harrison Dillard, world's record-breaking hurdler turned sprinter, created the unforgettable drama of the 1948 Olympic Games. Showing a clean pair of heels to the world's fastest speed merchants, he sprinted to victory in the 100-meter event in Olympic record time!

Harrison Dillard, just as he had dreamed so many years before, had won a coveted Olympic crown. A great hurdler, thwarted at his own specialty, had vindicated his honor as a sports hero—by winning not as a hurdler, but as a runner. No victory could have been sweeter, no conquest more richly deserved.

Of course, Harrison Dillard returned to America a genuine hero in the eyes of the world's track fans. Then, to prove his true greatness, Old Bones returned to his former specialty and began a new series of triumphs—again as a hurdler. And for years, he continued to run the hurdles undefeated—proving conclusively that he was still the world's greatest hurdler!

JOE DiMAGGIO

The Yankee Clipper

WHEN JOE DIMAGGIO played baseball for his high school in San Francisco as a boy of 14, he stood out from the other members of his team because he was the only one who didn't wear a uniform. As the son of a humble fisherman with eight hungry children to feed, Joe could not afford such a foolish expense as a baseball suit.

In spite of the boy's appearance, there was something about the tall skinny Joe that impressed his coach. One day he said to the youngster, "If you put your mind to it, Joe, you can be a fine ballplayer. Maybe some day you might even get to play for the San Francisco Seals."

Joe mumbled something under his breath. The Seals, as any San Francisco boy knew, was the greatest team in the world. Where did his crazy coach get the idea he'd ever be good enough for such a club?

A little later, Joe was playing ball for a team in the Industrial League, and getting paid for it, too. Now another problem faced him. What should he do? Go on playing ball for money or stay in school a while longer?

Joe's older brother solved that problem in a hurry. "You stay in school," he warned, "or I'll punch your ears off."

So Joe continued with his schooling. But baseball was under his skin and in his blood. One day a baseball scout caught Joe with his eye glued to a knothole at the Seals' ballpark. "Come on in with me," said the scout. "If you can play ball, maybe I can even get you a workout with the team tomorrow morning."

"You're kidding," said Joe. "They wouldn't want me."

But they did. Before long, Joe DiMaggio was signed to a contract by the Seals. He was only

18 at the time. In his first season with the Seals, he set a Pacific Coast record for hitting safely in consecutive games.

Three years later, Joe was in the big leagues as a center fielder for the New York Yankees. For 15 years, the fisherman's son was one of the authentic stars of baseball, winning the batting crown twice and in 1941, setting a major-league record for consecutive game hitting at 56! As a fielder and base-runner, he was unsurpassed.

No, Joe's high school coach had not been crazy for predicting that the boy would some day get to play for the Seals. Not only did the poor fisherman's son do that, he eventually rose to be the highest paid ballplayer in history, earning at the peak of his career the tremendous salary of $100,000 per year. And when he quit the game at 37 he did so in spite of the money he was getting. For Joe DiMaggio was too proud to continue taking $100,000 a year when he felt he could no longer produce the kind of baseball that the world had come to expect of him.

GERTRUDE EDERLE

Wonderful Trudy

SOME YEARS AGO, Gertrude Ederle was a chunky, laughing girl playing in the dirty streets of New York's West Side. One of a brood of many children, she was raised in a typical railroad flat that was situated over her father's meat market.

Trudy, as she was called, had one great love. Nothing made her happier than to dive into deep water and swim through it with grace and speed. And when she reached an age when most girls dream of dresses and parties, she became possessed with a wild idea. She would swim the English Channel, and become the first woman to do so.

Only five men in the world's history had been able to swim across the "sleeve" or La Manche, as the French called it. But Gertrude Ederle was determined to try it. When she was 19—in 1926—she quietly slipped off to Europe to run her dream to earth.

The natives of the little village of Cap Gris Nez on the French coast were startled one wet and miserable afternoon to see an old man slowly and carefully smearing grease over the body of a powerfully-built American girl on their beach. When he finished his task, the old trainer nodded to the girl and whispered, "Good luck." Gertrude Ederle smiled in answer. A moment later, she walked slowly and deliberately into the icy, lashing waters of the Channel. She was off on her great adventure.

Once in the sea, Trudy cut through the treacherous water with powerful strokes. Mockingly, the sea slapped back at her again and again, as though to tell her how rash she was to attempt so foolhardy a stunt. On she forged, through the waves, through the icy seas and currents. Dusk fell, night slipped into dawn. The hours passed and still the girl plowed along. Grimly she stuck to her appointed task, determined to win or go down in the struggle. At times her mind clouded over from the merciless beating she was taking from the angry waves, but she refused to give up.

At last, the end of the epic struggle came. After 14 hours and 31 minutes in the water, her foot struck firm ground. And, like a ghost, Gertrude Ederle staggered from the water to the pebble beach of Kingsdown on the English coast. She had triumphed over the English Channel!

Word of her feat electrified the world. The first woman to swim the English Channel had not only done what no woman in history had accomplished before but she had done it faster than any of the male swimmers who had successfully made the crossing since 1875!

When she came home to New York, she was the most famous and most talked-about woman in the world. That unassuming and modest girl received a tumultuous welcome to match any ever seen. Her path from the boat to City Hall was strewn knee deep in ticker tape as the world's largest city went wild over its own daughter. More than a million people turned out on the streets to cheer her. Trudy was went on for days for the 19-year-old girl who, overnight, had become the most famous woman of the day.

RAY EWRY

The Human Frog

FOR A TOPNOTCH ATHLETE to win an Olympic Games championship is a memorable feat. To win two Olympic crowns is a shining record for the history books. To win three Olympic crowns entitles an athlete to list himself among the immortals of sport. In all Olympic Games history only five super-human athletes were able to win as many as four Olympic championships. The incredible Paavo Nurmi is a giant among Olympic athletes for winning the astounding total of seven Olympic crowns. But, the greatest Olympian of all was Ray C. Ewry. A fact little known or remembered is that this American holds the record of winning more Olympic championships than any other man in history. He won ten Olympic crowns!

Ewry was a New Yorker by birth, but it was at Purdue University where this tall and lanky athlete first made his bid for track glory.

It was in 1900 that Ewry participated in his first Olympic Games. This international festival for the world's greatest athletes took place in Paris that year, and Ray covered himself with glory by winning three events—the standing high jump, the standing broad jump, and the standing hop, step and jump.

In 1904, the Olympic Games were staged in St. Louis, and again Ray was on hand to compete in his specialties. Once again, he won the standing high jump, the standing broad jump and the standing hop, step and jump. Now, the amazing New Yorker had six Olympic championships.

But six Olympic crowns was not enough glory for this "human frog"! In the next Olympic Games staged in 1906 at Athens, Greece, Ewry won two more Olympic championships in his specialties. Now, he had eight Olympic crowns.

However, Ray was not yet done with Olympic fame. For when the 1908 Olympic Games were staged in London, England, there was Ray Ewry, again playing the part of a "human frog." Once again he captured victory in two of his specialties—the standing broad jump and the standing high jump.

It was only then that this athlete, wearing the colors of the U.S.A., rested content. At last he was satisfied with his fantastic series of Olympic triumphs—ten Olympic championships, a record for individual accomplishments which remains unequaled in modern Olympic Games history!

The record alone makes a remarkable story. But even more astounding is the fact that Ewry didn't start competing in Olympic Games until he was twenty-seven years old, and still more incredible is the fact that the greatest Olympian of all time was an invalid as a boy. He was so sickly that once his life was despaired of, but the family doctor advised the lad to take up jumping to help build himself into a normal boy. The rest is history.

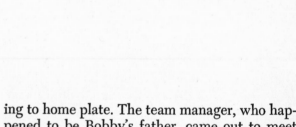

BOB FELLER
Bullet Bob

WHEN ROBERT FELLER was a boy of only 9, his father bought him a baseball uniform and took him out to the cow pasture on the family farm near Van Meter, Iowa. "Son," said Mr. Feller to his boy, "let's see how far you can throw a baseball." And he handed Bobby a regulation league ball.

Little Bobby reared back and let fly. The ball sailed a distance of 200 feet. Bobby's father let out a gasp of surprise. Then he made a momentous decision. He himself had once played semipro ball. His son, he decided, would be trained and prepared for the big leagues, nothing less.

From that day on, father and son spent many hours in the cow pasture throwing the baseball back and forth. When the boy would tire, the two would sit in the shade of a tree and the father would recount stories and legends about the game.

A year or two later, Bobby was playing shortstop for the kid team of his home town. One day, the boy playing first base let out a howl of protest, threw down his glove, and came storm-

ing to home plate. The team manager, who happened to be Bobby's father, came out to meet him. "What's the matter?" he asked.

"That Bobby!" squawked the young first baseman. "I'm not going to play if he's goin' to throw that hard to me. Looka my hands, he's bustin' 'em all to pieces!"

There was only one thing for the manager to do and, wisely, he did it. Bobby was moved from shortstop to the mound to become a pitcher. Without realizing it, he had taken his first step toward sports immortality.

The boy from Van Meter, Iowa, could throw a ball with terrific speed. At the age of 12, he came up with a curve ball that was a dazzler. He discovered it one afternoon in the cow pasture when one of his pitches suddenly dipped and broke three of his father's ribs.

When he was 15, Bobby was pitching for the grown-ups. One day, he was on the hill against a fast semi-pro team. In the stand sat Larry Gilbert, a major league scout. The scout's eyes almost popped out of his head when he saw

38

young Bobby's smoking fast ball. When the game ended, he rushed to where the boy was being congratulated by his friends and offered him a chance to sign up with New Orleans on the spot. When Bobby learned that the pay would be $1,800 a year, his jaw dropped open. "I'll take it!" he gasped.

However, the New Orleans Pelicans were not anxious to take on a boy so young, even if he could, as Gilbert insisted, throw a ball through a brick wall. Again fate intervened. New Orleans was a farm club of the Cleveland Indians, and before too long Steve O'Neill, Indian manager at the time, heard the wondrous news about young Bob Feller, speed-ball phenomenon. And when Cleveland met St. Louis, he brought Bobby in to give him a three-inning try against the Browns.

All Bobby did was strike out eight Brownies to get his nine outs in the three innings. And he stayed with the Indians from that moment, never spending so much as a day with any minor league team.

He was still a boy of 17 when he made his first start in the major leagues against Washington in 1936. The young farm boy pitched a masterpiece in which he mowed down 15 Senators on strikes on the way to victory. Later the same season, Bobby struck out 17 men in a game with his blinding speed. And a fabulous career in baseball was under way. The years that were to pass would see Bobby Feller smash one record after another. When he was 19, he struck

out 18 Detroit Tigers in a nine-inning game, setting a modern record. In 1946, he struck out 348 batters, a season mark. Over the years, he threw eleven one-hit games. And in spite of the fact that he spent four years in the Navy during World War II, he passed the magic 200-mark in victories in 1950. Since he entered the service when he was at the very peak of his powers, it may fairly be assumed that the four years he lost cost the fireballing Feller from Iowa another hundred victories.

Even more remarkable than his strikeout marks and his one-hitters are Feller's no-hit games. Bobby pitched three such classics in the major leagues. And one of those no-hitters was carved out on Opening Day of the 1940 season, a most remarkable feat. No other pitcher in history ever hurled a winning no-hitter on Opening Day.

With the passage of time, the zip went out of Bobby Feller's fast ball, but the loss of his biggest and most feared weapon did not stop the great Cleveland pitcher's phenomenal winning of baseball games. Substituting guile for speed and a good curve for sheer power, Feller continued to pile up victories. And his salary kept pace, going up and up until he reached a point where he was the highest-paid pitcher in baseball history. Sure of a future niche in baseball's Hall of Fame, the former Iowa farm boy must be ranked with the great pitchers of all time, a mound star of the first magnitude, who unquestionably is the greatest hurler of his generation.

BOB FITZSIMMONS

The Australian Blacksmith

ROBERT FITZSIMMONS, a blacksmith from Australia, was one of the most remarkable fighters ever to lace on a pair of boxing gloves. Although he was never more than a middleweight, he fought for and won three world titles in three different classes. They were the light-heavy and heavyweight crowns, as well as the middleweight title which he never lost in the ring.

He was already 36 years old, and the middleweight champion of the world, when he met James J. Corbett, the heavyweight title-holder for the biggest prize in boxing. Weighing barely 160 pounds, Ruby Robert knocked out the clever champion. After that, when he was 41 years old, Fitz went on to win the light-heavyweight title.

Fitzsimmons presented an odd picture as he stood in the ring waiting for a contest to begin. What little hair there was on his head was red. He had enormous shoulders and long python-like arms covered from wrist to shoulder with big red freckles. And his legs were like pipestems, long and thin.

Fitz rarely met men of his own weight in the ring. His boast was, in his own famous words, that "the bigger they are the harder they fall." And it was his paralyzing solar plexus punch that brought many an opponent down to his own level of size. It was the most feared punch in ring history.

One of the important points about the amazing career of Ruby Robert Fitzsimmons was that he was the first man ever to hold three different ring titles. He did not win them in order. He moved from the middleweight to the heavyweight and then back to the light-heavyweight titles. In every class there were none who could withstand the hammering blows from those long piston-like arms of his.

And there was no more colorful character than Ruby Robert in the boxing game. He was very fond of pets and had a number of them at one time or another. Most unusual of them all was the pet lion with which he loved to promenade through the streets. Nor would Fitz ever go to training camp before a fight unless his pet lion was with him to keep him company.

All in all, Bob Fitzsimmons fought over 350 fights in the ring. Despite the many murderous battles in which he engaged, so clever was the tall Australian that he bore not a single scar as evidence of them. And his career, beginning with his amateur days in New Zealand, lasted for 35 years.

Nothing is more remarkable about the great champion of three divisions than the last item in his long ring history. For Bob Fitzsimmons fought his last fight in the year 1914. He went six rounds against a big young heavyweight, a powerful puncher—and Ruby Robert was 52 years old when he did so!

THE FOUR HORSEMEN
OF NOTRE DAME

IT MAY SEEM ODD to consider as a single immortal of sports the four distinct individuals who made up Notre Dame's greatest backfield. But that is what they were, four different persons fused together into a single unit. On the gridiron, the four men operated as one mind with four bodies, all driving with smooth and closely-meshed perfection to win for Notre Dame.

The legend of the "Four Horsemen" began when four unknown youngsters first came out for Knute Rockne's Notre Dame football team. The immortal Rockne was not overly impressed at first sight with any one of them. Measured by gridiron standards, not one looked like a potential football star. Elmer Layden was a lanky, somewhat skinny, lad of 162 pounds. Don Miller was a studious youth of 160 pounds. James Crowley was a wise-cracking kid who tipped the beam at a bare 159 pounds. And Harry Stuhldreher was an alert, fast-thinking little fellow who weighed a rousing 155 pounds, dripping wet.

It was strictly an inspiration for Rockne to bunch the four youngsters into a single backfield. The 162-pound Laydon became the bruising fullback. Crowley at 159 and Miller at 160 became the halfbacks. And the 155-pound Stuhldreher became quarterback and field general of the Notre Dame football team.

Nothing like this quartet had ever been seen before on the gridirons of the land. What they lacked in beef, the four players made up for in tremendous speed, artful agility, deadly blocking a perfect coordination of their individual talents. For three glorious years, the Four Horsemen rode roughshod over the greatest college football teams from coast to coast. They made the All-America teams. College football, during their career, became big business. Tremendous crowds packed the football stadiums wherever they played. And during the three years, Notre Dame lost only two games and won two national championships!

Even after their gridiron days were over, the Four Horsemen managed to sparkle as they

41

went on to fame and fortune in their later lives. Don Miller became a celebrated lawyer and a prominent judge. Elmer Layden became football coach at his alma mater and then Commissioner of the National Football League. Jimmy Crowley too became a successful football coach at Fordham and later President of the All-American Football League. And little Harry Stuhldreher, sparkplug of the Four Horsemen, became head football coach at Wisconsin.

At last report, all four men had deserted the sports scene to become highly successful businessmen. The decades have passed since the Four Horsemen of Notre Dame roamed the gridirons of the land, but the memory of their exploits will be forever green wherever football is played and loved.

LOU GEHRIG

The Iron Horse

THE YEARS that have passed since his untimely death have failed to dim the memory of Lou Gehrig, the quiet hero who played so long and so well for the New York Yankees. There are so many things to remember about the great first baseman and home-run slugger!

Lou, a boy from the sidewalks of New York, was a football star at Columbia University when his mother who had labored for years as a cook suddenly fell ill. In order to obtain the money for the serious operation she needed, Lou left school to accept a $1,500 bonus from the New York Yankees.

He was just an awkward though powerful youngster when he first reported to the Yankees. But Gehrig worked with deep concentration to improve his skill. Nevertheless, it looked as though Gehrig might ride the bench for many months. The Yankees had Wally Pipp, an established star, at first base.

One afternoon Pipp reported to manager Miller Huggins with a bad headache. Huggins was sympathetic. "Take a couple of aspirins," he advised. "I'll put the kid on first today, and you can get back tomorrow when you feel better."

But Pipp never did get his job back. On the day he got his historic headache, Lou Gehrig started the most fantastic streak of day-in, day-out play ever run up by a ballplayer. For 15 long years, the durable Iron Horse of baseball played every Yankee game until he had run up the incredible consecutive game record of 2,130. Through the years, Gehrig shrugged off injury after injury to stay in the game—chipped bones, broken fingers and toes, wrenched shoulders, lumbago attacks, beanings failed to halt his ever-mounting record.

As the years sped by, Lou Gehrig became the idol of young America. Although he had the misfortune to play all his life in the shadow of baseball's greatest slugger, Babe Ruth, he set an awesome flock of records of his own. Once he hit four home runs in four consecutive times at bat in a single nine-inning game. Another time he banged out three homers in a single contest. Lou amassed a total of 23 home runs hit with the bases full. Altogether he hit 493 fourmasters, a total bettered by only three men in baseball, and ran up a lifetime batting average of .340.

One day, Lou Gehrig was stricken by a mysterious illness. Slowly his big body began to fail. There came an afternoon in Yankee Stadium when Lou stood in the middle of the diamond and bowed his head at the thunderous ovation that came to him from 70,000 saddened fans who had come to do him homage. It was the Iron Horse's last good-bye to the game he loved.

"I've had my share of good things," he said, weeping. "I'm the luckiest fellow in the world."

Luckiest indeed! Two scant years later, Lou Gehrig was dead at 38. His life had been short but his deeds had been mighty. The quiet hero with the big bat and the heart of iron left behind him a legacy of devotion to baseball that will not be forgotten.

GEORGE GIPP
One for the Gipper

To play the last game of his college career, George Gipp rose from a sickbed. It was a bitter-cold and snowy day. He pleaded with Rockne to let him play—to let him play for the last time. In the packed stands, the crowd set up a howl for the Gipper. Rockne relented and sent George out on the field. In the few minutes he played, he played brilliantly and scored a winning touchdown.

When George Gipp returned to the campus, he was seriously ill and was put to bed at once. He was never to leave that bed.

As he lay dying, Rockne brought him the news that he had been chosen for the All-America and that several major league teams were bidding for his services as a ballplayer. The Gipper smiled feebly in response.

"You're in a tough spot," said Knute Rockne to the sick boy.

"I'm ready," replied Gipp. "I'm not afraid to go."

"You'll get well, George," whispered Rock. "All you have to do is hang on."

George Gipp shook his head sadly. "No, Coach," he said. "I'll never make it. Will you do one last thing for me, Coach? Some time, when the team's up against it, when things aren't breaking right, tell the boys to go and win just one for the Gipper. Wherever I'll be, Coach, I'll know about it. And it'll make me very happy."

As the entire Notre Dame student body knelt in the snow outside the Gipper's window and prayed for him, the great football star passed away. At that moment, the legend of "One for the Gipper!" began. In years to come, Rockne was to win many games with George Gipp's deathbed message. And many a youngster has made his way to Notre Dame because it was there that George Gipp achieved immortality.

THE GREATEST and most colorful football player ever to attend Notre Dame was George Gipp. So deep an impression did he make on Notre Dame football that even after his death, and for many years, he helped the Fighting Irish win games as the ghostly "12th man" on the field of play.

"The Gipper," as he was called, was Knute Rockne's favorite player, though he was at the same time his most troublesome one. For, sad to say, George Gipp, a minister's son, was hardly a model for young America. His style of living was reckless and wild. He loved fun and mischief. The great back was also a gambler, capable of doing more with a deck of cards than a magician. His weakness for gambling and his seeming indifference to the serious side of life almost drove coach Rockne wild.

But once on the football field none could buck a line, or knife through tackle, or hip-weave his way to a touchdown, like George Gipp. He could pass, kick, or run to perfection. And he made everything look easy.

George hated discipline, and on several occasions was almost expelled from Notre Dame. But Rockne always saved him from the fate he deserved. The many intercessions by Rockne on the Gipper's behalf put the Notre Dame halfback deeply in his coach's debt. And the Gipper paid that debt with his life.

FRANK GOTCH
King of Wrestlers

ON A FARM near the little town of Humboldt, Iowa, a young and handsome giant named Frank Gotch worked long and weary hours trying to scratch a living from the soil. One day, he heard that it was possible to earn a little money as a professional wrestler. Since he was considered the strongest man in Humboldt, Frank decided to take a little time out from farming to see what he could do on the mat.

His first match as a wrestler brought young Frank Gotch fifty dollars for his efforts. It wasn't much, but it beat farming. It led Frank Gotch to devote the next 14 years of his life to wrestling. Combining brain, brawn and skill, he built himself into the greatest wrestling champion of all time!

Gotch's reputation grew fast. From all parts of the world came the outstanding wrestlers in the business to challenge the Iowa grappler. He defeated them all. For ten years he ruled as the wrestling champion of the world, and this was in the days when wrestling was a serious sport. Over all, Frank wrestled in 400 bouts—and lost but six!

As the idol of millions in the United States, Canada and Mexico, Gotch made wrestling a big-time sport in his day. As a matter of fact, he drew larger audiences than did the heavyweight champion of boxing when defending his title. The night Gotch defeated the fabulous George Hackenschmidt the first time, the largest crowd ever to see a wrestling match attended. The record gate which totaled over $100,000 has never been equalled to this day—and that happened over 40 years ago!

By the time Frank was ready to return to his farm, he had earned about half-a-million dollars—a great fortune in those days. Added to that were the honors that Gotch had won over the years. Babies had been named in his honor, as had buildings, toys, farm implements and a hundred other things. The word "Gotch" was a synonym for quality and strength.

The end for Frank Gotch was as cruel as his career had been glorious. The beautifully-muscled Frank Gotch, one of the strongest men in the world, was suddenly stricken with a mysterious disease. His fine body was reduced to skin and bones. He was only a skeleton, a shadow of his former magnificent self, when finally he closed his weary eyes.

When news of his death reached the people of his native Iowa, the whole state went into mourning. In Humboldt, his home town, every store closed down, the schoolhouse was shuttered and empty, on the day of his funeral. Thousands of weeping mourners, gathered from many parts of the land, trudged the icy path to the little rural cemetery on a cold December day to bid a final farewell to the farm boy who had been the greatest wrestling champion in history.

RED GRANGE

The Galloping Ghost

ALTHOUGH over a quarter of a century has passed since he played, Harold (Red) Grange is still accepted as the greatest broken-field runner in football. During the three years he played at halfback for the University of Illinois, Grange ran up an awesome total of yardage gained in carrying the ball. And so much did he capture the imagination of the public that record crowds turned out whenever Illinois appeared. When he became a professional, it was the same story—the magnetic and swift-running ghost brought out the first 70,000-crowd in the history of the play-for-pay game.

There was little in Red Grange's childhood that gave promise of the greatness to come. When he was 8, he seemed doomed to a life of inactivity, for the Grange family doctor told his father that young Harold had a bad heart and should be kept from playing any strenuous games whatever!

But somehow, Red outgrew his physical shortcomings. As a schoolboy at Wheaton, Illinois, he won 16 letters in football, baseball, basketball and track. As a college player, Red was to put his little home town on the map when he worked as a helper on an ice truck during summer vacations and came to be known far and wide as "The Wheaton Iceman."

He was a big, modest kid when he first entered the University of Illinois as a freshman with an athletic scholarship. Turning out for football, he saw 200 other candidates for the team. Red's first impulse was to pack up and go home. He didn't see himself competing with the big gang of huskies already out for the squad.

And Red's beginning was pretty much what he expected. The kid who had done so well at Wheaton seemed completely unable to run at all. He was so bewildered and tongue-tied that he could not explain why. Soon enough, however, the reason was discovered. Someone had issued the big boy from Wheaton a pair of shoes that were much too small for him. Every step he had to take was accompanied by excruciating pain!

When they finally gave Red Grange a proper pair of shoes, the coaches at Illinois began to see things. For there was no stopping the Galloping Ghost once he had a football in his hands. The first time in a frosh-varsity scrimmage that he returned a punt he sifted through the entire varsity to a touchdown, and Bob Zuppke, varsity coach, tabbed the boy as a future great.

The records that Red Grange set as a college player have never been surpassed. From the very first time he stepped on the gridiron for Illinois he was a sensation. Playing 20 games in three years for the Fighting Illini, Grange scored 31 touchdowns and gained over two miles of ground, a record that will probably stand as long as football is played. One of his finest achievements came on October 18, 1924, at the formal dedication of the vast new Memorial Stadium. With 69,000 spectators on hand, Grange handled the ball five times against Michigan in the first 12 minutes of the game—and made four touchdowns!

Grange played his last game for Illinois in 1925. He had been selected All-American three times, in 1923, 1924, and 1925. And when he left the campus, the number 77 which he had worn as a player there was retired forever in honor of the greatest back the university had ever had.

The sensational Galloping Ghost then became a professional. Here again, his appearance on the scene revitalized the pro sport. To begin with, he earned a cool $12,000 for the first

afternoon he played with the Chicago Bears. Then the great runner went on a tour of the nation playing football against all-star teams and attracting huge crowds to see him cavort on the gridiron. The Galloping Ghost picked up $100,000 a season for a couple of years as the professional sport of football took hold with the public through his efforts.

As a pro, Grange was a new sensation. Although he was still the great runner he had always been, Red won new respect for his phenomenal defensive ability, being selected before all other backfield men as the finest defensive back in the game. Grange played professionally for 10 years before quitting the game to become a highly successful radio and television broadcaster of college and professional football.

There have been few backs like Red Grange in the long history of American football. Fast, elusive, a genius of evasion and pace, the redhead from Illinois awakened a whole world to the glory of the gridiron. It is from the era of Red Grange, the Galloping Ghost, that the game can measure its growth to the point where it is now one of our greatest spectator sports. Like all the others in other fields who made the 1920's the Golden Age of Sport, Red Grange was cast in a heroic mold. Apparently the mold was broken, for his like has not been seen since.

RALPH GREENLEAF
Man With a Cue Stick

TO THE MILLIONS who play pocket billiards, the champion of champions has always been Ralph Greenleaf. In his chosen sport, Greenleaf stood out from the others much as Babe Ruth did in baseball. And it was thanks to his brilliance at the green-covered tables that pocket billiards became a headline sport.

Ralph Greenleaf became a pocket billiard player because of the delicacy of his health as a child. Born in Monmouth, Illinois, he was kept indoors much more than most boys his age. His doctors had warned that he was not to participate in any of the usual strenuous games of other boys.

To keep him amused, Ralph's family bought him a small pocket billiard table as a sort of toy to play with. It became more than a toy to the intense youngster. By the time he was 8 years old, he could beat anyone of whatever age in the whole town of Monmouth.

When Ralph was about 12, Bennie Allen, world's pocket billiard champion, passed through Monmouth and for his own amusement agreed to a match against the youngster. Taunted by some of the locals that the boy wonder would beat him, Allen made a sizable wager that he would prevail. Much to his astonishment—and chagrin—young Ralph Greenleaf beat him handily.

The news of that stunning defeat made headlines across the country. Ralph Greenleaf became the new boy wonder of sports. A couple of years later, when he was 14, the Monmouth cue wizard took on Johnny Layton, new world's pocket billiard champion, and beat him too, in a winner-take-all encounter.

Five years later—when he was 19—Ralph Greenleaf won his first world's pocket billiard championship, and did it without the loss of a single match through the tournament. The sensational nature of his play galvanized interest in the sport. Greenleaf made world tours, arousing enthusiasm for the game everywhere as he took on and beat all comers. He became a popular sports hero and his skillful play created many boisterous demonstrations to the point where he even was carried away from the table on the shoulders of his fans after an especially notable victory.

All in all, Ralph Greenleaf won 19 world's pocket billiard championships, many of them in succession. His title conquest in 1929 was marked by a run of 126 to take the crown in only two innings, a record that has never been beaten in tournament play. Another time, in a match, Greenleaf made a run of 167 to set another record. His best mark, 269, was made in an exhibition match.

The boy wonder of pocket billiards rose quickly to fame and greatness. It was also the fate of this great artist with the cue to pass from the scene while still at the height of his powers at the relatively early age of 50. But a champion he was for nearly 40 of those 50 years —and his equal as a pocket billiard player may never be seen again.

WALTER HAGEN

The Haig

THE STORY of Walter Hagen, one of the world's great golfers, is full of contradictions. He became a golfer because he was so good a ballplayer. The less he practiced, the better he played. And the more he earned from his fabulous skill as a golfer, the less he could hang on to.

Hagen started in sports as a baseball player, and he was so good that in his youth more than one major league club sought his services. As great a judge of baseball talent as John McGraw said that Hagen as a golfer was a great ballplayer gone to waste. But fate took a hand in Hagen's life right at the start. A star with his high school baseball team, he needed money to get a new glove and a pair of spiked shoes. To earn the dollars he needed, Hagen hired out as a caddy at a nearby golf links. And there the clever and resourceful Walter Hagen decided that golf could offer him a larger stage for his talents and a place where he could strut alone before the world. So Walter Hagen became a golfer.

For three decades, Walter roamed the tournament circuit and, over the years, his colorful personality made him the darling of the sports scene. Everywhere his name became a symbol of great playing skill. And how he traveled! Always accompanying him were a valet, a private secretary and a personal caddy. And because he always took along a half-dozen trunks packed full of dazzling clothes, he became known as the Beau Brummell of golf. Among his friends in all parts of the globe he counted kings and princes, lords and ministers, the bluebloods of aristocracy and wealth. They all wanted to play golf with Walter Hagen!

And what a golfer he was! Not only was he the most colorful golfer the game has ever known but also one of its greatest champions. In his time, he won 65 major golf tournaments, among which were included the United States Open twice, the British Open four times, and the Professional Golfers Association championship an unprecedented five times!

Gay, relaxed and friendly away from the golf links, Hagen was a veritable man of ice once a match began. No one was more arrogant and cold-blooded in competition. No one could withstand better the pressure of a close match for a big stake. It is told that once he came to play for the first time at a certain tough American golf course. He had been promised a fee of $25,000 only if he won. But upon his arrival, Hagen refused to go out even to inspect the course before the match. Instead, he sent out his caddy to look it over—he stayed in the clubhouse chatting with friends! An hour later, Walter Hagen went out and broke the course record!

He was the first golfer to earn a million dollars from the game, but all of it slipped through his hands—for there was nothing he enjoyed more than gay living and good fellowship. That was Walter Hagen. He lived as daringly as he played, to carve his niche in sports history as the fabulous "Haig"—the greatest golf pro of them all!

PUDGE HEFFELFINGER
Pudge of the Gridiron

FOR OVER HALF a century the name of Pudge Heffelfinger has been spoken with awe by football followers. In the dim, early days of intercollegiate football, Pudge was the roughest, toughest, most durable guard in the game.

Pudge Heffelfinger was first bitten by the football bug as a youngster in Minneapolis. Scion of a wealthy and prominent family in that city, young Pudge, fired by what he could read about the gridiron exploits of the Big Three, headed unerringly for Yale and football glory. And it was in 1888 that Yale's famous playing coach, Pa Corbin, first laid eyes on the man who was to become the Eli's greatest lineman.

Pudge, as a green freshman, went out for Yale football in hopes of becoming a back on the squad, as he had been on the high-school team he had organized in Minneapolis. But the Yale coach informed him that the team needed linemen, and ordered him to play guard. Heffelfinger took his place in the line opposite the powerful varsity team and Corbin roared out, "All right, let's see if this kid has what it takes!"

The veteran Yale players happily proceeded to give the ambitious young freshman a joyous initiation to Yale football. They kicked him in the shins, hit him in the midriff, smashed his nose, cracked him sharply over the knuckles, trampled on his fingers, and gave him an all-over shellacking. The youngster from Minnesota took all the punishment without complaint, soaking it up like a sponge and coming back for more.

After an hour or so of this, the Yale coach shook his head sadly. "You're too good-natured, Pudge!" he shouted. "If you want to play Yale football, you'll have to be mean and bang 'em back!"

So Pudge Heffelfinger hitched up his moleskins and got rough. By the end of that first day of practice he had made the Yale varsity line. And he played every minute of every game thereafter, as long as he was at Yale.

Although he weighed as little as 186 pounds in his heyday, Pudge Heffelfinger became the most feared football opponent of his era. As football's first roving guard on some of Yale's greatest teams, Pudge spread fear and havoc in enemy ranks. And, while the tremendous Yale offense rolled up 698 points in that first season Pudge played, not a single point was scored against the Blue line led by Heffelfinger and his mates. With Pudge roaming the line, leading the interference, shifting with the enemy backfield, opposing teams considered themselves lucky to find themselves still on the field at the close of a game. For three straight years, Pudge was selected on Walter Camp's All-America team. To his dying day, Camp always hailed the Yale guard as the greatest in his position in football history.

How rugged and tough Heffelfinger was is indicated in other ways, too. Where others quit the game after graduation, Pudge never gave up the game. In 1916, some 25 years after he had played his last game for Yale, Pudge returned to the Yale campus at coach Tad Jones' request just to pep up the fine team Yale had that year. Pudge got into uniform—at the age of 49!—and lined up with the scrubs against the Blue varsity. What he did to that good varsity team was a caution. He flattened half a dozen men including a couple of All-Americas half his age, broke a few of their ribs, and generally battered the varsity into bruised submission. Coach Jones finally—but politely—invited the elderly Mr. Heffelfinger to leave the field and confine his loyal efforts to vocal rather than physical support.

When he was 53, Pudge played a full 60 minutes of rough football against the Ohio State All-Stars, in a game filled with famous young ex-college players of the day—and he more than held his own in that scintillating company. "I'd have done better," he said after the game, "if I hadn't dislocated my shoulder right after the opening kickoff."

Nor did Pudge give up playing football even then. He played his last game at the unbelievable age of 65—and played on the winning side.

It was not until he reached the ripe old age of 86, that the Grim Reaper finally brought down football's greatest linesman.

Golden Girl

SONJA HENIE

SONJA HENIE got her first pair of skates when she was six by insisting that she would accept no other present from her father for Christmas. Within a week, the determined little girl had worn the skates out. She immediately demanded—and got—another pair.

Hour after hour, day after day, the little girl skated up and down the ice near her home in Oslo, Norway, in imitation of her older brother and his friends. Her father, a world's champion cyclist, helped her and encouraged her. And, in just two years, she was able to skate rings around her brother. The little girl was on her way to fame—and a fortune she could hardly have dreamed of.

Sonja delighted the world with the beauty and precision of her figure skating when she began to compete in public. But she was more than a skater to the sports world. Noted as a horsewoman, hockey player, swimmer and sprinter, she also won 18 skiing championships and three Scandinavian tennis titles. It was only because she became such a superb figure skater that most of her other sports were given up.

At 14, she won her first figure-skating title, the Norwegian national championship. Then, in 1926, she competed in the world championship and finished second. She was never again to taste defeat. The next year in Oslo, she won the first of her ten consecutive championships of the world. Then, in 1928, 1932, and 1936, she won three Olympic figure skating championships in a row against the best from everywhere.

With no new worlds to conquer in competition, Sonja turned to professional figure skating. Her first appearance as a pro was only a stunt in connection with a movie she was making, her debut in films. She merely did a few numbers between the periods of a hockey game. It didn't create a sensation—but a fabulous new career was under way. Soon she was drawing big crowds to watch her perform. Everyone wanted to see the lovely Norwegian miss do her breathtaking feats on ice. The money began to pour in. And Sonja Henie became the first girl athlete to earn a million dollars.

For twenty years, the name of Sonja Henie shone brightly in lights all over the world. Skating in ice shows and in the movies over the two decades, she grossed fantastic earnings of many millions. Truly did the determined little skater from Norway become the golden girl of sports!

THOMAS HITCHCOCK, JR.

Tommy on a Horse

TOMMY HITCHCOCK was born with a silver spoon in his mouth. When he first reached a hand out of his cradle, they stuck a polo mallet into it instead of a rattle, so the saying goes. And when he was old enough to walk, they put him on the back of a horse and made him ride. At 13, he was a first-class polo player. At 16, he was an established star. Before he reached voting age, he was acknowledged to be the greatest player of his time.

To be a ten-goal player in polo is to be a top man in the sport. Only a handful have been so rated down through the years. Tommy Hitchcock, like his father before him, was a ten-goal player. But like no one else in history, he remained a ten-goal player for 18 years of national and international play.

Tommy brought to polo a flaming drive and a slashing style that all but turned the game upside down. What is more, he opened the game, a rich man's sport, to the outside world by bringing in good players, regardless of their background. When he added a couple of Texas cowboys to the international squad he formed with them a team that stayed unbeaten for years.

Tommy was a firebrand in polo, nor was he any less so in life. When World War I broke out, he was a youth of 17. Too young to join the American fighting forces, he went to France where he became a flyer with the famous Lafayette Escadrille. Almost immediately he shot down three German planes and received the Croix de Guerre from a grateful French government.

Then one day he was himself shot down in flames behind the enemy lines. Taken prisoner, he was shipped to a prison camp. On the way, he leaped out of a speeding train and made his way on foot to neutral Switzerland, a distance of 100 miles.

At the end of that war, Hitchcock returned to polo. For years he played on America's international team, and was one of the most brilliant defenders of the coveted Westchester Cup against all English challenges.

When World War II came along, there was no holding Tommy Hitchcock in check. Although well past 40, he made himself a place in the United States Air Force. As a lieutenant colonel, he was a combat flyer and commander of a flight group. Then came tragedy. In a training flight over Salisbury, England, the fate that had dogged his steps so many years finally caught up with Tommy Hitchcock. The man who had been a polo star at 13, a wartime aviation hero at 17, the world's greatest polo player at 20, died in a plane crash as an active combat flyer at the age of 44. Tommy Hitchcock was every inch a hero—in life as well as in sports!

BEN HOGAN
Little Ben

LIFE WAS BITTER for Ben Hogan when he was a boy. Son of the town's blacksmith and junk dealer, he grew up in Dublin, Texas, a skinny and unhappy kid. When his father died, little Ben, aged 9, went to work. He delivered newspapers, ran errands, did whatever he could to earn a few pennies to help out. When he was 12, he hired out as a caddy on a golf course.

The game of golf fascinated the boy. He spent hours watching the players. Soon he was trying to play himself. At every opportunity, he pestered the older boys and the club members with questions about the game.

Little Ben became a terrible nuisance to the others on the golf course. Once, to shut him up, he was dumped into a barrel, nailed in, and rolled down a steep hill. Ben was almost killed by the cruel prank.

But he insisted on playing golf and learning everything he could about the game. He skimped and saved. Then, 19 years old and as skinny as ever, he found he had amassed the fine sum of $75. He was ready to become a professional golfer himself!

At Phoenix, Arizona, Ben entered a tournament and won $50 as prize money. He went on to San Antonio and picked up another $88. Then he went through three more tournaments without gaining a cent. When he got to the Los Angeles Open, Ben had exactly fifteen cents between himself and the world. He played the three days of the tournament living on nothing but oranges for breakfast, lunch and dinner.

For years, Ben struggled along, getting nowhere. After seven years on the pro golf circuit, he still had nothing in fame or fortune. It was 1938. Hogan was entered in the Oakland Open. On the eve of the tournament, he got married. To his bride, he made a heartbreaking promise.

"Valerie," he said, "if I don't win anything here, we'll go back to Texas, and I'll give up golf for good."

But Ben won $380 in that Oakland Open. It wasn't much, but it was the turning point in his career. He began to win, and he continued winning until he had won four National Open championships, two Professional Golf Association championships, and captured two Masters tournaments. Over one stretch of time, Ben Hogan finished in the money in 41 consecutive tournaments. As a professional golfer, he became the biggest money-winner of all time.

In 1949, at the height of his fame, Ben Hogan was injured in a near-fatal auto accident. He wound up in a hospital more dead than alive. There was serious doubt whether he would walk again. But less than a year later, Hogan staged one of the greatest comebacks in sports, as he moved into big-time golf again. His courageous comeback brought him to the highest peak of glory of his whole career. In one year—1953—when Ben was 41, he won the United States Open, the British Open, and the Augusta Masters, to become the first man in history to win all three in a single year.

WILLIE HOPPE
The Boy Wonder

THERE HAVE BEEN all kinds of champions in the world of sports, and a handful of them have created extraordinary records of triumph in their pursuit of glory. But no champion has dominated his sport so completely for such an incredible span of time as Willie Hoppe.

The first chapter of his story took place way back before the turn of the century. In back of a barber shop, a solemn-eyed six-year-old boy stood on a wooden box beside a rickety old billiard table. The boy's head was barely above the level of the table. Standing at his side, the boy's stern old German father placed a miniature billiard cue into the hands of his small son. And Willie Hoppe received his first lesson in the game which he was going to make his own for half a century.

Little Willie learned to play billiards so quickly and so well that his father sold the barber shop soon after the boy's eighth birthday in order to take his *wunderkind* on a barnstorming tour of the United States. Along with them went Mrs. Hoppe, as a sort of traveling schoolmistress.

Willie was barely 18 when he sailed to France to meet the supposedly invincible Maurice Vignaux, billiard champion of the world. Vignaux

had insisted that there be a side bet of $1,000 and that the winner take all gate receipts. Hoppe accepted the conditions, raised the money for the side bet, and made his way to France.

The match between the American "Boy Wonder" and the renowned "Old Lion" of France stirred up much excitement on two continents. The shy and nervous boy met the smiling and confident old master in the glittering ballroom of the Grand Hotel in Paris before a select audience of world celebrities. Over the cables flowed every detail of the match as it progressed. Millions all over the world followed the match and millions of francs were bet on the final outcome as it went on.

The result of the meeting between the old master and the young challenger created a world sensation. For Willie Hoppe won the historic match and became the champion of the world. The date was January 15, 1906. Hoppe's career lay before him.

From that day on, the news of his exploits became a staple of sports headlines. No name was more familiar to the man in the street, no face better known as it gazed calmly out of the sports pages of papers from one end of the earth to the other. He met challengers from Europe, from America, from Asia, from every land on the face of the globe where billiards was played—and always he emerged victorious, always he prevailed as champion.

The fabulous years of the Golden Age of Sports arrived and passed gloriously. Great names in many sports rose to glory, burned their way across the sports sky, faded and disappeared. Babe Ruth for one; Bobby Jones, Jack Dempsey, Bill Tilden, Ty Cobb, Jim Thorpe for others. They all made their indelible mark, then became memories and entries in the dusty record books. Only one name burned as brightly after their passing as it had before their coming on the scene—that of Willie Hoppe, a champion before, during, and after the Golden Age of Sports.

As the years passed, the saga of the grand old man became more and more amazing. Nothing seemed able to stop the steady march of victory. The Boy Wonder grew old with years, weary with gruelling competition, slow with time and age. But never did he falter, never did he relinquish his jealously-guarded title as billard champion of all the world!

In 46 years of first-line competition, Hoppe won and held a world's title in billards 51 times. No champion in any sport so monopolized the top spot in his game. Under the terrific tension of tournament play, his eye stayed as keen, his hand as steady, his competitive spirit as firm as when he first had stepped into big time play as a boy of 18. Only when he reached the age of 65 did he at last reluctantly rack up his cue and withdraw from the grim ordeal of day-in, day-out championship struggle. He was already a legend in sports, a living memory who had stubbornly stayed at the top in billiards for nearly half a century.

It has been estimated that Hoppe, over the years, spent more than 100,000 hours at the billiard table and had walked some 26,000 miles in his pursuit of one championship or another. When he retired, Hoppe could look back 59 years to that day in his father's barber shop when he first held a cue in his hands. From that far-off beginning to the day he gave up competitive billiards, Willie Hoppe, one-time Boy Wonder of the billiard world, had been the perennial master of all he surveyed, the most durable champion in any sport at any time!

ROGERS HORNSBY

The Rajah

HE WAS ONLY A pinked-cheeked 19-year-old when he left the Denison club in the bush leagues to report to St. Louis and the Cardinals at the tail-end of the 1915 season. When he arrived at the St. Louis ball park, he introduced himself to manager Miller Huggins.

"What position did you play at Denison?" the little manager asked.

"Second base," replied Hornsby.

"What did you hit?"

".277."

"That isn't much," commented Huggins.

"I'm sure I can do better than that," said bashful Rogers Hornsby. "Give me a chance and you'll see."

But he didn't. Hornsby batted a mere .246 during the last 18 days of the National League season. On the last day, the young and somewhat naive Hornsby approached the manager in the clubhouse.

"What do you think of me, Mr. Huggins?" he asked.

"You're a fine fielder," answered Hug. "You've lots of hustle but you've still got a lot to learn about hitting. I guess I better put you out on a farm."

"Oh, you don't have to do that," protested Hornsby. "I can go to my father's farm."

When Hug stopped laughing at the young man's lack of understanding, he thought the matter over—and decided to keep Hornsby with the club. Thus began the story of the incredible career of baseball's all-time greatest right-handed hitter.

For that was what Rogers Hornsby turned out to be. The records he ran up eventually were to land him in baseball's Hall of Fame. Over 24 seasons, he led the National League in batting seven times, six of them in succession. Three times he batted .400 or better, including a fantastic .424 in 1924, highest ever recorded in the modern game. And his lifetime average was a glittering .358, a figure second in all baseball only to the total made by the incomparable Ty Cobb!

And there was nothing puny about the hits the great slugger drove out. He led the league several times in home runs and runs batted in, and made a record for the National League of hitting 12 home runs with the bases full.

As a player, nothing in the world existed in the heart and mind of Rogers Hornsby but baseball. The game was his god and he worshiped it with single-minded devotion. During his playing days he avoided reading or going to movies for fear of hurting in some way his keen batting eye. And he wouldn't talk about or listen to any subject other than baseball. It was all he lived for, the only thing he cared about.

Though he started as a $200-a-month player, the Rajah worked his salary up to the $50,000-mark before completing his playing days, and earned over half-a-million dollars during his career.

That career was a hectic one. He played for five different teams and managed five different teams. He led the St. Louis Cardinals to their first pennant in 1926, and then drove them to a World Series triumph over the lordly New York Yankees.

Superb as both player and manager, Hornsby nevertheless had his difficulties as a leader. Always a perfectionist and a driver of himself, the Rajah tried to get from his players the same single-minded devotion to the game and the same level of ability he had himself displayed on the field. He was sharp-tongued and stern at all times and some players came to resent his cold and direct bluntness. But others were devoted to him as a leader and particularly as a teacher. There are many in baseball today who learned how to hit and field from the stern-faced Rajah. And just as he could not tolerate the shortcomings of his players, he was not afraid to speak his mind to those in authority over him. There is a well-authenticated story about

Hornsby facing up to the redoubtable John Mc-Graw himself. McGraw once berated one of Hornsby's teammates for making an error during a game and the Rajah interceded sharply on the player's behalf. This incident was one of the reasons why McGraw saw fit to trade Hornsby away after one season with the New York Giants. All Hornsby had done that year was play 155 games, bat .361, score 133 runs, and drive in 125!

Rogers Hornsby's life has been a series of ups and downs. His lack of patience with players, his demand for perfection, have shunted him back and forth from one club to another over the years. But Hornsby the player must never be forgotten. With all his remarkable batting records, he was also a superb fielder, being especially proficient at making the double play, so vital to a second baseman. He could cover a lot of ground and knew how to play every hitter in the league.

As the greatest right-handed slugger of them all, Rogers Hornsby deserves the accolade given him by experts of baseball as one of the great second baseman in baseball history. Whatever he said or did, no one can take that away from the incomparable Rogers Hornsby!

DON HUTSON

Man With the Magnetic Mitts

FROM THE VERY FIRST DAY, some 25 years ago, when he stepped out on the football field of the University of Alabama, Don Hutson was marked for fame as the greatest pass receiver and scoring threat in history. After a glorious career with the Crimson Tide as the receiving half of the famous Howell-Hutson axis, as an All-American, and as the star of a memorable Rose Bowl victory over Stanford, Don entered the professional ranks. He joined the Green Bay Packers, one of the great pro aggregations in the National Football League. And with the Packers Don really blossomed out, setting records by the dozen and establishing all sorts of marks for future players to match if they could.

Don Hutson came to the Green Bay Packers in 1935 and stayed with them until 1945. For 8 of the 11 seasons, he led the National Football League in receiving passes. Fast, big, and with an uncanny knack for being in the right spot at the right time, Don was an impossible man to defend against. Often, an opposing team would put three men against him to try to break up

the passes that came his way. But it never made the slightest bit of difference how many men guarded the Packers' flying end with the magnetic mitts. He outfeinted them, outran them, outguessed them, and left them sprawling on the turf as he skipped down the field with the pigskin under his arm.

The records that Hutson set over the years are many and fantastic. Only one man, Sammy Baugh, ever set more. Among the marks that Don put up for the rest of the league to shoot at are: most points scored, 825; most passes caught, 489, of which 101 went for touchdowns. He caught 4 touchdown passes in a single game. He gained 8,010 yards on passes and in one season, 1942, set a mark of 1,211 yards gained. He scored in every one of 41 consecutive games and led the league five times in scoring.

Besides being the biggest scoring threat whenever he was on the field of play, Don could do a lot of other things. In 1943, he won the field goal kicking championship of the league. And as a defensive halfback throughout his long career, Don was unsurpassed.

With the inimitable Don Hutson at end, Green Bay was one of the greatest teams in pro football, winning six league championships. There were many other stars on that team, but none could compare with the tall, slim, swift Hutson. A measure of his true greatness can be made by noting the fact that in the one year when every opposing team put at least two men on Don to keep his glue-like fingers from latching on to passes from the Green Bay backfield, the one-time Alabama star set a record for touchdown passes caught in one season with 17! And an additional note that does as much to explain the genius of Don Hutson's versatility and adaptibility to the circumstances of the moment is the record that he holds for the *shortest* touchdown pass ever caught in a professional football game—four inches!

WALTER JOHNSON

The Big Train

Walter Johnson pitched for Washington 21 years. The Senators were a chronic second-division ballclub through most of them but the Big Train's feats as a pitcher border on the incredible. He won a total of 413 games, more than any other hurler in American League history. He struck out 3,497, a record for all baseball. For 10 consecutive seasons, he won 20 or more games. One year, he won 36 and walked only 38 men. Another year he won 16 in a row, equaling a record. And he pitched the most consecutive scoreless innings, 56!

It was in his second season, that of 1909, that Walter Johnson suddenly leaped into the headlines as baseball's greatest hurler. In September, on a Friday, Johnson pitched the Senators to a 4–0 shutout over the New York Yankees, letting them down with five measly hits. The next day, Saturday, Johnson again faced the Yankees, this time shutting them out, 6–0, with three hits. Sunday, at that time, was a day of rest for baseball, so Johnson just rested. On Monday he went out and beat the Yankees, 4–0, giving them two hits. Johnson had performed the incredible feat of winning three consecutive games in four days, all of them shutouts! All that on a salary of $2,700 a year!

It was only after 17 years in the majors that Walter Johnson got his first chance to appear in a World Series. The Senators met the New York Giants, and a world of baseball fans wept with joy when the old master, in the twilight of his career, won the seventh and deciding game of the Series to bring the world championship to Washington. It was a fitting climax to all the years in which victory had come his way so often in a losing cause!

THERE IS NOTHING more useless to a ball club than a damaged catcher. When the Washington Senators' regular backstop broke a finger in June 1907, the club manager decided to send him to far-off Idaho to scout a young pitcher about whom a Washington traveling salesman had been bombarding him with letters. The catcher went out to take a look, watched the big, ungainly poultry-farm boy lose a 1–0 heartbreaker in 12 innings, and then signed him for $100 to a Washington contract. The catcher had never in all his life seen a man throw a ball with such speed.

Walter Johnson arrived in Washington wearing a derby hat and carrying a cardboard suitcase. They laughed at the big hayseed with the arms that seemed to dangle to his knees. But he stayed on to become one of the greatest pitchers in baseball.

The Big Train, they came to call him, and his first experience as a major league pitcher was one to make a man of iron quail. He was ordered to the mound to face the pennant-bound Detroit Tigers with such murderous sluggers as Ty Cobb and Sam Crawford in the line-up. Johnson allowed only six hits, three of them bunts, and though he lost the game, 3–2, he was on his way to fame.

BOBBY JONES
Immortal Golfer

ever seen on a golf course. He could not tolerate defeat. When things went wrong for him, he flew into a blistering rage and smashed his golf clubs, raved, ranted, even cried. But never did he let up in his quest for golfing perfection.

Bobby Jones made of his boyhood years a time of dedicated loneliness. While other children were engaged in the usual variety of activities, Bobby was on the golf course, practicing hour after hour by himself.

The promise was always there and the future seemed almost assured. At eleven, Bobby played his first round of golf in 80 strokes. A couple of years later, Bobby, still a high-strung and excitable boy, qualified for the Southern Amateur championship. And, at 14 years of age, he finally won his first important tournament, the Georgia State Amateur championship, and went on to compete in his first National Amateur tourney.

Somewhere along the line, Bobby Jones finally learned how to control his mercurial temper. Perhaps it was because his game had become so good that he did not need to punish himself any longer. Or maybe it was because the boy had matured generally. In any case, Bobby did succeed in conquering himself—and in so doing, he conquered the world of golf as well.

THE ONLY QUARREL there can be about Bobby Jones is whether he was the greatest golfer of all time or just the greatest amateur golfer the world has ever known. There is no doubt that the man who fashioned the incredible Grand Slam of golf in 1930 belongs among the towering giants of the game.

Robert T. Jones, Jr., to give him his full name, was born a sickly child with a serious stomach disorder. His doctors in Atlanta, Georgia, gave him little hope for a career in sports. Nevertheless, Bobby outgrew his sickness, and it was a chubby and excitable little boy of nine who won his first golf championship, the Junior Cup of the Atlanta Athletic Club in 1911.

That was the beginning of a fantastic career. At the very start, and for years to come, Bobby displayed one of the most ferocious tempers

The list of Bobby's accomplishments is a shining scroll of great victories over man and golf courses. In eight years, he won thirteen major championships on both sides of the Atlantic. The United States Amateur title fell to him five times, a record that may well stand forever. Four times he won the United States Open against the best amateur and professional players in the world. And to them he added the British Open three times and the British Amateur.

It was just another exhibition match that started Jones on his way to the climax of his career and the accomplishment that still defies comparison in the realm of golf. The match was arranged between Jones, then reigning as National Open and Amateur champion and the colorful professional, Walter Hagen. Jones, of course, played merely for the sake of winning if he could. But Hagen had been guaranteed a fee of $5,000 for the match. And the story is that he had wagered twice that sum on himself to win over the young champion from Georgia.

Jones, playing for his honor and reputation, did the best he could, which was plenty good. But Hagen, his eye on the rich monetary reward, played with cold and calculating magnificence. The result was that Bobby took the worst shellacking of his life. The two men never met on the links again.

The humiliating defeat rankled in Bobby's heart. For a long time he sought some way to wipe out the ignominy of the licking he had received from Walter Hagen. At last came the opportunity not only to eradicate the memory of a crushing defeat but also to inscribe his name once and for all among the immortals of golf.

The year was 1930. Bobby was still a youthful 28. He went to England and won the British Open championship at Hoylake. Then he swept the field to win the British Amateur at famed and ancient St. Andrews.

Home again, Bobby went to Interlachen and won the National Open. The world was buzzing with his feats now. Who had ever heard of a man sweeping three such great tournaments in succession? But there was still one more important goal before Bobby Jones. The United States National Amateur was to take place at Merion. No one had ever come close to winning all four national championships. Could Bobby Jones win the fourth and make the Grand Slam of golf?

Bobby could and did. At last he stood on the very pinnacle of golfing greatness. There was nothing left for him to conquer, nothing more to win in all the world of golf. Bobby Jones reigned supreme, the greatest golfer in the world, the man who had pulled off the incredible Grand Slam of golf. His magnificent feat had never been achieved by any other man—nor is it likely that it ever will be.

The triumphant Jones withdrew from competitive golf and returned to his native Georgia. Through the years he had grown to be calm, quiet, sure of himself. But with him went immortality. No man who can sweep four national championships in a single year can ever be forgotten as long as golf is played.

JOHN B. KELLY

America's First Oar

JOHN B. KELLY was born before the turn of the century at a time when rowing was one of America's most popular sports. Oarsmen were the idols of the public in the 90's, and even the newspapers of the day gave big headlines to the stories of rowing victories when no other sport was even mentioned on the back pages.

For Kelly, who earned his living humbly as a bricklayer in and around Philadelphia, rowing in single sculls became a passion. And the object of that passion was to win the Championship Single Sculls, the top race for oarsmen in America.

John B. Kelly, after scoring a number of minor successes on the water, finally achieved his ambition in 1919. Then, for the first time in the history of that event, he repeated the feat the following year. In the same years, 1919 and 1920, he won the Quarter-Mile Single Sculls, an exceptionally gruelling sprint race for individual oarsmen.

With nothing left to conquer in this country, John Kelly looked elsewhere for competition. He made application to compete in the most hallowed rowing race in the world, the Diamond Sculls at Henley-on-Thames in England.

Kelly waited patiently for his application to be accepted but, to his consternation and bitter disappointment, it was coldly turned down without explanation. And then Kelly learned from unofficial sources that because he had been a bricklayer and therefore was not a "gentleman" oarsman, he was not eligible for the race.

The snobbery of this action infuriated the

American champion oarsman, but there was little he could do about breaking through the Henley ban. He went to Antwerp, Belgium, and won the 1920 Olympic sculling championship for the United States. He went to Paris in 1924 and won both singles and doubles events. But, in spite of those glorious victories, the refusal of the Henley authorities to let him row in the Diamond Sculls continued to rankle in his heart. He determined to avenge the insult somehow, some time, at the first opportunity that offered. And he would have his vengeance at Henley, come what might.

Kelly waited 27 years to get his wish. In 1947, John B. Kelly took his son, John, Jr., to England for the Henley Regatta. The boy had won the Championship Single Sculls in America the year before. Trained, taught, and inspired by his father, the boy had become, in his turn, the greatest oarsman in America. And at Henley-on-Thames, he brought his father the vengeance he had so long dreamed of by winning the Diamond Single Sculls at the age of 19. In 1949, the boy repeated the brilliant triumph over the world's greatest rowers. Nor was that all. For the boy showed himself to be as great an oarsman as his father by capturing the Championship Single Sculls five times, the Quarter-Mile Single Sculls twice.

As proud as the great old sculler was of his son, nothing that he did, nothing he could have done, gave John B. Kelly, the three-time Olympic champion and America's finest single scull oarsman, more pleasure than the youngster's victory in the race that had once been barred to him because he had been a common bricklayer.

The Michigan Assassin

STANLEY KETCHEL

WHENEVER A FIGHTER wins the middle-weight championship of the world, the second richest crown in boxing, invariably his stature as a fist fighter is compared with Stanley Ketchel, the greatest middleweight of them all. For although the fabulous "Michigan Assassin" has been gone from this earth for more than four decades, he is still the measuring rod for all middleweights.

Stanley Ketchel first stepped into a prize ring in 1903. He was only 17 years old, but it was immediately apparent that in boxing a new meteor had flamed across the sky. Born on a dismal Michigan farm, of Polish descent, Stanislaus Kiecal ran away from home when only 15, to ride the rods of freight trains and live in the jungles of hoboland. A footloose wanderer of the road, the boy learned to fight in the hobo jungles where there was no other way to survive. And he had learned well.

In the ring there were few who could withstand the blazing two-fisted attack of this youngster. His whirlwind onslaught was so devastating that in his first 39 ring encounters, Ketchel knocked out 35 opponents. That was why they nicknamed him the Michigan Assassin.

He was not yet 21 when in a furious bloody battle that went 32 rounds, he knocked out Joe Thomas and became the new middleweight champion of the world. Handsome, gay and tough, Stanley Ketchel became the most glamorous and most popular fighter of the time—the idol of millions.

Ketchel fought the famous Philadelphia Jack O'Brien, one of the cleverest of all light-heavyweight champions, and he licked him. Once, he pitted himself against Jack Johnson, for the heavyweight championship of the world. But although in that furious famous battle in 1909, Ketchel was finally knocked out in the 12th round, he came close to winning, for with a single mighty blow he had floored the huge Johnson, who was one of the greatest of all heavyweight champions.

At the peak of his career as middleweight champion of the world, the Michigan Assassin agreed to meet his persistent rival for the crown, a rugged battler named Billy Papke. As the opening bell clanged, Ketchel walked out to the center of the ring to shake hands with his opponent. But Papke surprised the champion. Instead of accepting the proffered glove, Papke swung from the heels—and connected.

Jarred by the unexpected blow, Ketchel fought twelve bloody rounds, purely from instinct for he was in a complete daze, before the treacherous Papke finally stopped him, and captured his middleweight crown.

Ketchel, furious, challenged Papke to a return match. He laughed at the tradition that no champion ever before had recovered a lost title. He wagered most of his purse that he would.

As the return match started, a few weeks later, Ketchel did not make the mistake of offering to shake hands. Fighting with cold fury, the Michigan Assassin gave Papke one of the worst beatings ever seen in a ring. Finally, he stopped the slaughter in the 11th round when he knocked the bloody Papke out. Papke left the ring so battered and bruised that when they brought him home his own family failed to recognize him.

Stanley Ketchel had made history by becoming the first middleweight to recover a lost title. More than that, he had established himself as the greatest of middleweight champions.

While only 24 and still the middleweight champion of the world, fate stepped in to take a hand in the blazing career of Stanley Ketchel. Ironically enough the fabulous Michigan Assassin of the ring, came to a violent and untimely end outside the ring—by assassination. On October 10, 1910, while breakfasting alone on a lonely farm in Conway, Missouri, he was shot fatally in the back by a jealous farmhand.

BILL KLEM
He Never Called One Wrong

WILLIAM J. KLEM is the man who, in his own words, "never missed one" in 36 years of major league umpiring. There has never been a more famous umpire. His appearance, his walk, his voice, his manner of calling a play or waving a player to the showers, were all distinctive and characteristic.

When Bill Klem started calling them, baseball was in the era of "Don't argue with the umpire—sock him!" It was thanks to Klem that baseball got rid of a great deal of its rowdyism and became as clean and sportsmanlike as it is.

Klem began as an umpire in the Connecticut League back in 1902. He had failed to make much impression as a player in the minor leagues before he accepted the offer to don the blue suit. In his first week on the new job, Klem ran into the most notorious umpire-baiter in the league. From the moment the game began, the player ragged Klem unmercifully, squawking on every play. As the game proceeded, the arguing became more and more bitter, with Klem sticking to his guns and shouting the heckler down. When the game ended, all stood by to see the angry player light into Klem with his fists. As the player approached him, Klem stood waiting for the first blow to fall. But there was no fight. When the player reached Klem, he stuck out his hand with a grin on his face. "Young feller," he said, "I just want you to know you umpired a great game. Let's be pals!"

It was in his first year up with the major leagues that Klem set the fashion for umpires to stop enraged ballplayers. As one of them came running at him with fire in his eye, Klem drew a line on the ground with his toe and calmly waited. As the player came near, Klem raised his hand. "If you want to stay in the game," he intoned, "don't cross the line!"

The player drew up short. From that day, no player dared cross a line Klem drew.

The respect in which Klem was held by the players was attested by the fact that he umpired in 18 World Series, a record. His absolute integrity, his sense of authority, brought dignity to his job. He introduced many innovations to the game over the years, all of which have become standard among umpires.

After 37 years of "calling 'em as he saw 'em" the greatest umpire of them all, quit his trade because of a woman. He had had a rough afternoon umpiring a ball game. Twice that day he had been struck by foul balls. As he walked off the field, a female fan said to him sympathetically, "You sure had a tough day, Pop!" That convinced Bill Klem that his day as an active umpire was done. The very next day, he retired.

By the time he was ready to call it a day, Klem had won the love and respect of everyone in baseball. Only he among all the umpires was ever honored by a special day in a big-league park. That was in 1949 at the Polo Grounds. The veteran umpire was given many gifts and a plaque from the sports writers. In response to the praise and applause, Klem made the remark that does more to describe him than any other.

"Baseball is more than a game to me," he said. "It's a religion!"

SUZANNE LENGLEN
La Grande Suzanne

FEW SPORTS FIGURES ever commanded more publicity than the glamorous French tennis star, Suzanne Lenglen. At the height of her fame, the unpredictable and temperamental star of the courts was the darling of tennis fans all over the world. It was not only because she was a superlative player that Lenglen created such a furore. Her stormy and erratic behavior made her the spoiled child of tennis, and the delight of followers of the game.

The Wimbledon title, symbolic of world supremacy in tennis, fell to the flashing racket of Suzanne six times between 1919 and 1925. Each time the crown was won with almost ridiculous ease by the colorful French star. And in 1925, she set an absolutely unbeatable record when she went through the entire All-England tournament without the loss of a single game!

For years she defeated the best players of her sex without extending herself. In fact, no player could even win a set from her. Mercurial and feather-footed on the court, Suzanne Lenglen could leap and pirouette with the skill of a ballet dancer. In the view of many experts, her peer as a tennis player among women has not yet been seen.

The great French star was on top of the world when she defeated the rising American player, Helen Wills, in 1926. And then something happened that changed the whole course of her life. That year, at Wimbledon, Lenglen kept a huge crowd, including Queen Mary herself, waiting for over an hour before she finally appeared to play her match. When she did arrive, there was a violent quarrel with the tournament officials. Refusing to play at all, Lenglen went home to Paris. The British were outraged by what they considered a snub to their Queen. The French leaped to their heroine's defense. The angry exchanges across the Channel grew hotter and hotter. An international incident seemed well on the way to serious proportions.

To put an end to the ill feeling between nations, Suzanne Lenglen turned professional. As such she became the star performer in the first touring tennis troupe of all time. Not only did she earn a fantastic sum of money by her efforts, but she also set the style for future amateurs by becoming a professional in quest of gold for her playing talents.

Suzanne Lenglen, however, paid with her life for the fame and fortune that came to her. When she was only 39 she fell ill and died. Her death certificate said that her passing was due to pernicious anemia. Those who had followed her long and hectic career were sure it was the unceasing, almost cruel, exploitation of her fantastic talents on the tennis court that had brought the world's most glamorous, most exciting lady of the courts to an early end.

BENNY LEONARD
Mama's Boy

did he engage in a match anywhere that he did not rush to the telephone as soon as it was over to talk to his mother and tell her he was all right. And nearly always it was a victory that he had to tell her about.

Benny's famous trademark was his habit of entering the ring with his hair carefully slicked down. Fascinated fans watched his shining head bob in and out, waiting for the hair to be mussed. But rarely did any one manage to displace a single hair. Usually he left the ring as unruffled and unmarked as he had entered it.

A superb boxer and a powerful hitter, Benny became lightweight champion of the world when he was barely 21 years of age. Once he had become king of his division, he took on all comers. Within two years, he engaged in 56 fights. For eight years he ruled the lightweight class with ease and eclat. When no worthy opponent remained on the scene to be licked in defense of his crown, he retired undefeated, one of the few champions in history to do so.

But the ring-fires burned fiercely in Benny Leonard. After a few years of soft and lazy living, he came out of retirement for another whirl at glory in the roped arena. This time, he fought as a welterweight. And for a while, the old "boxing master" gave the sports world a new thrill, as he scored victory after victory. But at last, he tasted defeat. When urged to hang up his gloves and leave the ring forever, Benny Leonard replied:

"Maybe I'm now too old to fight, but I'll remain in boxing till I breathe my last."

He kept his word. After he finally had retired as a boxer, he became a prize-fight referee. One night, while refereeing a boxing bout—Benny Leonard dropped dead!

He died as he had wished—in the center of a prize ring where in his glorious youth, he had won all his fame and his fortune as the greatest lightweight of them all!

BENNY LEONARD, the "boxing master" from New York's east side, became a prize fighter quite by accident. As a poor kid, Benny could never afford to pay his way in to see a fight. One night he was perched on a skylight atop a small-time boxing club eagerly watching the fight in the ring below. In his excitement, Benny lost his balance and crashed through the skylight. The irate promoter grabbed the boy before he could escape. And Benny, in order not to have to pay for the broken glass, offered to replace a boxer who had failed to show up for his bout that night. The promoter let the 16-year-old youngster go into the ring. Benny won his match. And a great career had begun.

His meteoric flight to the top really got under way when a new manager bought his contract —for one measly dollar. In time, Leonard earned more than a million dollars in the ring.

One of Leonard's most memorable traits was his devotion to his mother. Benny's feeling about her was genuine and touching. It soon brought him the nickname of "mama's boy" but it was a label that he wore with pride. Never

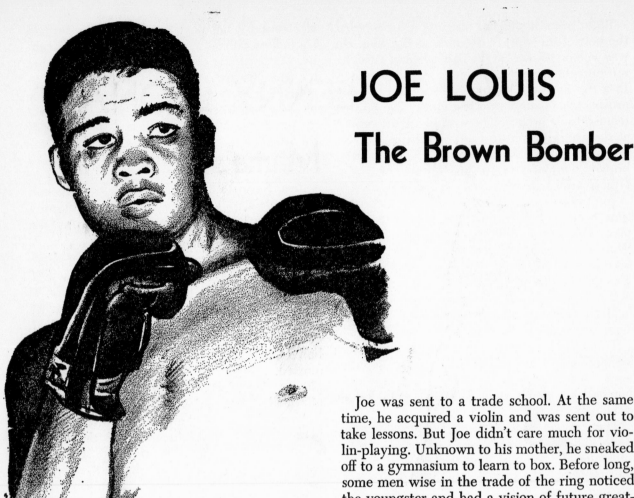

JOE LOUIS
The Brown Bomber

NO MAN had a more humble beginning than Joe Louis. He started life as Joseph Barrow in a shabby wooden shack in an Alabama cotton field and he lived his boyhood days in bitter poverty. He had little to eat, his Sunday suit was a pair of ragged overalls, his best shoes were torn rubber-soled sneakers. Nevertheless, before he turned 21, Joe was famous all over the world. And when he was 23, he was the heavyweight boxing champion of the world, the youngest boxer in history to hold that glittering title.

At an early age, Joe was brought to Detroit by his mother. At 16, he was one of thousands of Negro boys who roamed the slums of that city, and he seemed doomed to life-long obscurity. He left school in the fourth grade, barely able to write his name.

His mother worried about young Joe. She knew he was not qualified to do much because of his lack of education. But she wanted him to be more than an unskilled laborer. Perhaps, she thought, he could do something with his hands.

Joe was sent to a trade school. At the same time, he acquired a violin and was sent out to take lessons. But Joe didn't care much for violin-playing. Unknown to his mother, he sneaked off to a gymnasium to learn to box. Before long, some men wise in the trade of the ring noticed the youngster and had a vision of future greatness. They took him under their wing and began to shape him as a professional fighter.

What Joe Louis's potent hands have done in the squared circle is truly a saga of fistic history. Over the years, they earned him more than four million dollars. And they hammered out a sports legend of Joe Louis, the fighter and Joe Louis, the man.

For Joe Louis is probably the greatest heavyweight champion of all time. The record books tell the story in cold black and white statistics. In 1934, Joe fought his first professional fight, won it, and collected $50 as his end of the purse. From then on, no heavyweight engaged in more contests or scored more knockouts. As champion he wore the crown longer than any other title holder. He defended his title more times than all the other champions in history combined! He defeated 25 challengers for his crown. Added to that, no champion in history was ever more respected nor ever as much admired for his sportsmanship as Joe Louis was in the 11 years he held the title. Even the President of the United States became his friend.

Right from the start of his career, Joe toppled the best of the world's big men in the ring. He was well on his way to the title when in 1936, he ran into the former champion, Max Schmeling. In a terrific upset, Schmeling knocked out the prospective champion in 12 rounds. The bubble seemed to be broken. The world took to scoffing at the aspirations of the soft-spoken young Negro from Detroit. As for Schmeling, that beetle-browed German strutted and boasted with the typical arrogance of a conquering bully.

Joe Louis said nothing. He merely bided his time, waiting for a return match with the German. Only once did he express any feeling. Word came to him that Schmeling had said he was yellow. Joe broke out in anger. "You say 'Smellin'' calls me a quitter?" he exclaimed. "I'll tell you something. When we meet again, he'll go only one round. That's all, just one!" They met again in the ring two years later.

True to his word, Joe annihilated Max Schmeling in their return match in one of the most furious and most vicious beatings ever handed out in the ring. That massacre lasted only 124 seconds!

There never was a heavyweight champion quite like Joe Louis, simple, dignified, humble and honest. To his mother, he had said before his first fight, "If I ever do anything to disgrace my race, I hope I die!"

The sports scene has been filled with legendary figures who have gambled greatly with their names and fortunes, but it remained for Joe Louis, the humble colored boy from the Alabama cotton fields, to make the biggest bet of all. He did it not once but twice when he laid his million-dollar title on the line against nothing at all. Twice the Brown Bomber defended his heavyweight crown against dangerous opponents and refused to accept any money for his fistic services. Both times he gave his end of the purse to the Army and Navy Relief Funds. When some hard-boiled cynics expressed astonishment at a man who would dare to wager his priceless title against nothing in return, Joe Louis had an answer as simple and dignified as everything he said. "I'm not fighting for nothing," were his words. "I'm fighting for my country!"

Through the years, Joe did many kind things, kind and generous and thoughtful things, that never saw the light of day. He helped broken-down fighters, old people and children. It was not for nothing that a well-known writer said of him, "Joe is a credit to his race—the human race!"

There are innumerable stories that can be told about this remarkable man. Perhaps they can best be summed up in the short but eloquent tribute paid him by the fabulous former Mayor of New York, the late James J. Walker. At an important sports dinner one evening, before many celebrities from all walks of life, Walker rose to make a speech about the Brown Bomber. For once, the wise-cracking and colorful little New York Mayor spoke with dead seriousness. Pointing to Joe Louis who was seated near him, he simply said, "Joe, you placed a rose on Lincoln's grave!"

CONNIE MACK

Patriarch of the Dugout

IT SAYS A LOT about a man that he could manage one major league ball club for fifty years and then leave the dugout as the most beloved man in baseball. But that is the praise Connie Mack, born Cornelius McGillicuddy in the small village of East Brookfield, Massachusetts in 1862, earned for himself in the 67 years he was in baseball.

When the lanky, skinny McGillicuddy first broke into professional baseball as a catcher, he was a 22-year-old cobbler's assistant. So that his name would fit a boxscore, he shortened it to Connie Mack.

Mack played in the minors for three years before he was sold to Washington. His debut as a major league catcher was a sad one. In his first game he made six errors back of the plate. But he proved to be a real ballplayer in the days when baseball was a game mostly for roughnecks. He was as tough as rawhide. Connie Mack caught 664 games in the majors, as he combined managing and playing for the Pittsburgh Pirates. A broken leg cut short his career as a catcher, and after two years in the Smoky City, Connie Mack went to Philadelphia when the American League was organized, to manage the Athletics.

It was then that the saga of Connie Mack, the granddaddy of all big league managers, really began. From 1901, his first year at Philadelphia, until the close of the 1950 baseball season, when he was eighty-eight, Connie Mack was the Ath-

letics and the Athletics were Connie Mack. He helped build baseball from its early small beginnings to the national pastime it is today.

With skill, wisdom, understanding, patience, courage, heart and humor, Connie Mack, always gentlemanly in manner and soft in speech, developed some of the greatest teams in baseball history and many of the greatest stars in the game. Through his hands passed such immortal stars as Eddie Collins, Mickey Cochrane, Jimmy Foxx, Home-Run Baker, Jack Coombs, Eddie Plank, Chief Bender, Lefty Grove and Rube Waddell. Under his guidance, Philadelphia won nine pennants and five World Series. Some of the teams he piloted to championships were so mechanically perfect that victory became monotonous, and Connie Mack broke them up to start all over again. In all the years he managed the Athletics, he hardly ever spoke a harsh word to an erring player. "My good gracious" was his strongest epithet. No baseball man became so nationally loved and respected as that familiar figure of the tall, high-collared gentleman in the dugout waving his scorecard at his players out on the field.

Fifty years a manager of one major league club—a record that may stand for all baseball time—and sixty-seven years in baseball! There never will be another like Connie Mack.

CHRISTY MATHEWSON

Big Six

CHRISTY MATHEWSON was only 10 when he discovered that he possessed a skill which would in later years set him apart as the greatest control pitcher in all professional baseball. The son of a gentleman farmer, Christy had been born in 1880 at Factoryville, Pennsylvania. One of the things he loved to do when there were no chores or homework to occupy him, was to fling stones at objects within pitching distance. His accuracy, a natural thing, was remarkable. Then, somehow, he learned how to make a stone curve sharply in flight by flicking his wrist in a certain way. Soon he could hit his mark squarely regardless of whether he was throwing a straight or a curve pitch.

So accomplished did the boy Christy become that at 11 he was considered good enough to play ball with boys of 17 and 18. But whether he played or not, he constantly practiced, sometimes with his familiar stones, sometimes with a baseball.

The first time Christy stepped to the mound to pitch, he was paid the munificent sum of $1 for his services. And he had to walk six miles to get to the game—and six miles after it was over to get home again.

Matty entered Bucknell University when he was 17, and there proved to be an honor student and a star athlete. His mother had hopes of Christy becoming a minister. While he failed to follow his mother's desire, he remained deeply religious all his life. He never played a single game of baseball on Sunday, either at school or later as a professional.

Matty played football, basketball and baseball at Bucknell, and was also his class president, a member of the glee club, and active in several literary societies. Despite all his college activities, Matty managed to earn $200 a month playing baseball outside of school. Then, one day, he signed up for his first regular professional baseball job with Taunton in the New England League at a salary of $90 a month.

Matty went up to the big time when he was only 19. It is hard to say whether his pitching for the New York Giants made a greater impression on baseball men than his character. It is impossible to find fault with the great ace pitcher on either score.

Christy Mathewson pitched for 17 years in the big leagues. With the famous fadeaway pitch which made him famous, his uncanny control and tremendous speed, Matty won 373 games through the years, a National League record. He established another modern league record when he won 37 games in one season. On one occasion, he pitched 68 consecutive innings, the equivalent of 7½ games, without issuing a single base on balls, also a league record. And, though he pitched two no-hit, no-run games during his major league career, his most outstanding feat was that of hurling three shutouts in a single World Series, a mark that is unlikely ever to be matched.

But it is the figure of Christy Mathewson the man that clings closest to the memory of those who knew and loved the great hurler. Few men in baseball ever commanded the love, respect, even adoration, that Big Six, as baseball had nicknamed him, enjoyed all his life. His courage, his sense of honor, his unselfishness and modesty, made him a model for all the world to follow. Handsome, blond, a six-footer plus, he was always the perfect gentleman, soft-spoken and well-mannered. And his honesty was so

unquestionable that umpires would even take his word on decisions they had to make on the ball field.

Fate decreed that this wonderful man should fall ill at a relatively early age of tuberculosis. He had fought in World War I, gone overseas to France, and had been gassed. Valiantly, and for years, he fought the disease, the result of his gallant war services. He returned from a sanitarium to baseball briefly when he was 42 as part owner and president of the Boston Braves. Then one day he collapsed from overwork. The great Matty died on October 7, 1925. It was a sad day for baseball.

With his death, a true giant of baseball passed from the scene. The tradition of good sportsmanship and gentlemanly manners that he established will never fade. Matty will always hold a revered place, not only in the record books, but also in the hearts of baseball men the world over.

· HALL OF FAME ·

King of the Decathlon

BOB MATHIAS

ROBERT BRUCE MATHIAS was born in Tulare, California, on November 17, 1930. When his mother learned that he was not the daughter she had been hoping for, she cried.

Bob Mathias had a perfectly wretched childhood. Although he received the tenderest of care, he was anemic at seven, and seemed vulnerable to every juvenile disease that came along. At one time or another, he suffered from chicken pox, measles, whooping cough and scarlet fever. Nothing unpleasant passed him by.

For years, the boy lived on special diets to counteract the effects of nosebleed and anemia. Until he turned 13, he was obliged to take frequent naps every day in order to conserve his puny strength.

Gradually good care began to have its effect on little Bob Mathias—good care and plenty of play. The more he was able to play, the stronger he got. Suddenly, he began to shoot up. His eyes cleared, his arms and legs became firm and muscular.

By the time he was 17, Bob Mathias stood 6 feet, 2 inches tall and weighed 190 pounds. At high school, he had become an all-star at basketball, football and track. The boy who had been such a weakling had built himself to physical health. And, when the time came for him to enter his country's service, the United States Marine Corps found him to be an absolutely perfect specimen of manhood!

The city of Tulare, with its population of 12,000, knew long before the rest of the nation that it possessed in young Bob Mathias one of the world's remarkable athletes. Bob's exploits in football, basketball and track and field soon brought him wider attention. But it was not until the tryouts for the 1948 Olympics came along that he achieved some fame.

Bob sought a place on the United States Olympic squad. As an all-around athlete, his heart was set on getting into the decathlon, a trial in 10 tough events. His efforts were crowned with success. Bob was chosen to represent the United States in the most difficult and gruelling event in the Olympic Games.

At London, Bob met the all-around track and field stars from 20 nations. On the first day of the decathlon, he ran the 100-meter race in 11.2 seconds. He leaped just under 22 feet in the broad jump. He put the shot 42 feet, 9½ inches. In the high jump, he tied for first place, and then ran the 400-meter race in 0:51.7.

At the close of the first day, with five events completed, Bob Mathias stood third among the world's greatest decathlon men.

On the next day, London was a sea of rain and fog. Conditions under which the men were to compete were miserable. First came the pole vault. Bob soared over the bar at just under 12 feet. In the javelin throw, he made a mark of 164 feet. And he ran the heart-breaking 1500 meters in the gloomy darkness over a wet and clinging track.

Bob emerged from the rain and fog in first place, winner on his first try at the Olympic decathlon. All in all, he rang up the total of 7,139 points, only man in the competition to surpass the 7000-point figure.

With victory achieved, the place of Bob Mathias in the world of sports was acknowledged without question throughout the civilized world. When he entered the 1952 Olympic Games at Helsinki he was no longer an unknown, but a seasoned star of track and field. And again he won the decathlon, this time with a grand total of 7,887 points.

However, the fact that Bob Mathias won the Olympic decathlon twice in a row is not the outstanding point in the story of his athletic life. Nor is the fact that he became a great football star at Stanford where, as fullback, he led an undefeated team into the Rose Bowl. There is no doubt that he deserves plenty of credit for everything he has done in sports. But there is something else about Bob Mathias that is the most remarkable fact of them all. When he entered—and won—his first Olympic decathlon back in 1948 he was only a high school boy—17 years of age! Not only was he the baby of the United States team that year, he was also the youngest man ever to win an Olympic track and field championship!

She Bowled Them Over

FLORETTA D. McCUTCHEON

The champion protested. "Don't make me play a woman," he said. "She'll make me look bad."

"It's possible," was the answer. "But maybe not the way you think."

Jimmy Smith agreed to go on with the match. He bowled three strong games for a total score of 686—good enough to beat anybody, nine times out of ten.

But it wasn't good enough to beat the little housewife. Mrs. McCutcheon bowled three games for a total score of 704! The flabbergasted champion, when he recovered from the shock, called her the greatest bowler in the world—bar none!

When the story of the match got around, Mrs. McCutcheon was suddenly a celebrity. Everybody wanted to see her bowl. Soon she was traveling all over the country, giving exhibitions, competing in tournaments and matches. Along the way she made records for women's bowling that are indelibly inscribed in the record books. They include ten perfect 300 games; 9 games at 299; a three-game set for a total score of 832. Over a ten-year span of play against the toughest competition, Mrs. McCutcheon made a grand average of 201 for 8,076 games.

After shattering all the records, and setting a bunch of her own for others to shoot at, Mrs. McCutcheon, acknowledged by all to be the greatest woman bowler the game had ever seen, retired from competition in order to teach her skill to other women. Thanks to her untiring efforts, millions of women now find in bowling one of their most popular and successful sports.

UNTIL she was 33 years old, Floretta D. McCutcheon was merely a housewife in Pueblo, Colorado, and had never even heard of the sport of bowling. It was when she began to worry a little about her weight that a friend suggested that she try bowling as a reducing exercise.

The first time she tried to lift the 16-pound bowling ball, Mrs. McCutcheon was ready to quit. But she persisted. She watched others, saw how much smoothness and rhythm meant in the game. Soon she found herself managing quite well.

She had been bowling a couple of years or so when one of America's star bowlers, Jimmy Smith, eight years the national match champion, came to Pueblo to give an exhibition of his skill. The owner of the alleys where he was to play asked him whether he would care to meet one of the local players.

"Glad to," answered Smith. "Where is he?"

"She," corrected the alley-owner. "Meet Mrs. Floretta McCutcheon."

JOHN J. McGRAW

The Little Napoleon

NO MAN DID MORE to make baseball our national pastime than John McGraw. A five-foot seven-inch bundle of dynamite, McGraw exploded on the big league scene with a bang. In the 1890's, he was the game's finest third baseman with the legendary Baltimore Orioles. As manager of the New York Giants from 1902 to 1932, the McGraw touch was indelibly imprinted on baseball as a fine art.

McGraw's influence on the men who played for or against him was tremendous. No one could come close to the Little Napoleon without being affected by him in some way. Some loved him. As many more hated the very ground he walked on. It had to be one or the other. You couldn't ignore him or let him alone.

As a person, McGraw was a mass of contradictions. He could be generous, lovable, kind. He could also be a tyrant, abusive, mean. Whatever his mood or attitude to the players around him, some things were always constant. McGraw had raw courage, a burning determination to win at whatever cost. And he was shrewd and clever enough to get what he wanted.

McGraw was a pioneer in baseball. Creative and highly imaginative, he was responsible for many innovations in the game. He invented and developed the hit-and-run play that practically revolutionized the sport. He made an attack weapon of the bunt. McGraw was first to hire a player exclusively as a pinch-hitter. And long before the term was known, he was the first to employ the science of psychological warfare against an opponent to win games.

The firsts that must be credited to John McGraw are beyond reckoning. Here are a few. He taught his players that baseball was not a rough pastime but a dignified trade. He was the first manager to insist that players were entitled to all the salary they could get—and saw to it that they got it. He was the first pilot to arrange for his men to live in the best hotels instead of being kicked around in rooming houses as they had been. And it was due mainly to his efforts that ballplayers finally won the respect of the outside world as gentlemen.

When runty, white-faced John McGraw first came to New York as player-manager in the summer of 1902, the Giants were deep in last place. The little Irishman, stubborn, ambitious, tough, left New York, a sick and tired old man in the summer of 1932—and again the Giants were in last place. But during the 30 years between, John McGraw proved beyond doubt that he was the greatest manager the game of baseball ever saw. Seated in his specially built, raised chair in the dugout—he was the first manager to pilot from the bench—the Little Napoleon from his dugout throne earned himself the right to be known as the most colorful, the fightin'est, manager in major league history.

McGraw ruled his men with a fist of iron. Every decision was made by him, none by his players. Depending on his moods, he would send one player on to fame, banish another to oblivion. He would take eccentrics, numbskulls, broken-down has-beens, and bully them into becoming world-beaters. Whipping, driving like the master of a slave-ship, McGraw master-minded his Giants to ten National League pennants and three World Series championships. In the 1916 season he whiplashed his boys to a record 26 victories in a row, a mark that still stands. Four of his pennants were consecutive, the first time in history a manager performed such a feat in the majors.

No man could play under McGraw without being marked by the touch of the old master. He trained hundreds of rookies into magnificent ballplayers. And, at one time, half the managers in the two major leagues were the products of McGraw's iron stamp. Even the man who broke all records by winning five World Series in a row acknowledged his debt. Said Casey Stengel, leader of the New York Yankees, "Everything I know about baseball I learned from John Mc-Graw."

There never was a tougher loser than John McGraw, and no man ever drove so relentlessly and with such single-minded cruelty and heartlessness to win. But that was John McGraw on the ball field. Away from it, no manager ever did more gracious things for his old-time players. He got them good jobs. He staked them to new starts in life. For example, when old Amos Rusie, his once-great pitcher, fell on evil times, McGraw bought him a farm so the old fellow could live out his years without worry. When McGraw's famous third baseman, Eddie Grant, died in the service of his country—the only big leaguer to be killed in World War I—hard-boiled, heartless John McGraw continued to send Grant's family Eddie's regular pay checks as if the third baseman was still alive. And nobody ever knew—not from John McGraw!

John McGraw was many things to many men. But to baseball itself, he was truly a Giant, the heart and spirit of knock-down, drag-out competition, a genius of style and strategy, a leader beyond compare. And though his day is gone and his ways abandoned, John McGraw, last of the dugout swashbucklers, is still a man to remember for all the great things he did for our national pastime.

79

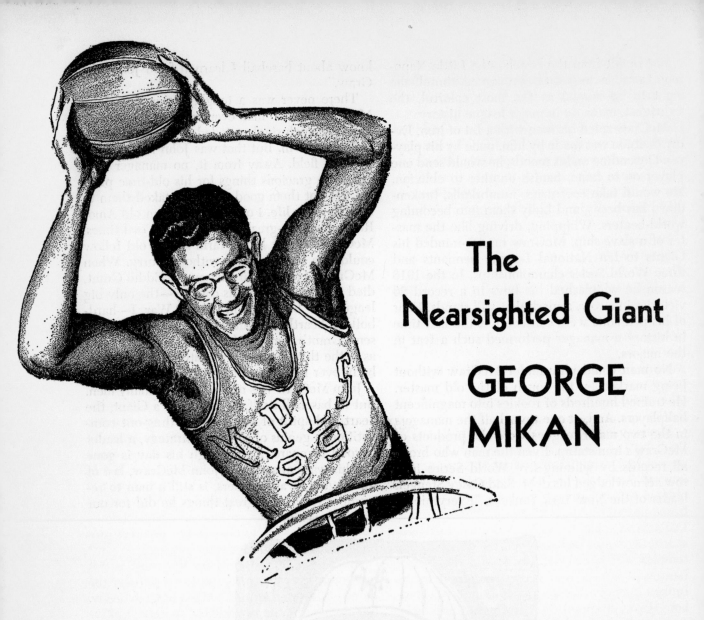

The Nearsighted Giant
GEORGE MIKAN

WHEN THE HISTORIANS of sport sat down to select the greatest basketball player of the first fifty years of this century, the vote, with hardly a dissent, went to a good-natured giant who had, for over a decade, been turning topsy-turvy all the records established since the beginnings of the game. The name of this paragon was George Mikan, 6–10 in height, 250 pounds in weight, who had, since his first ponderous efforts to toss a ball through a hoop at DePaul University, gone on to cut as wide a swathe in professional basketball as Babe Ruth had in baseball.

Mikan's first contact with the sport came when he was a small boy in Illinois. His father, after a career as a crack semi-pro pitcher, had opened a tavern in Joliet. George converted the spacious yard back of the Mikan home into a crude basketball court. There, with his pals of the neighborhood, he participated in rough-and-tumble basketball, while Grandma Mikan served as referee and enforced penalties for fouls with a sharply-swung broom. It was during one of these rather hectic scrambles in the backyard that he clumsily stepped on the ball and fell, breaking a leg. So serious was the fracture that the Mikans' doctor gloomily predicted that the boy would never again play basketball.

But George went on to high school and tried to make the basketball team. He failed miserably, for the coach found him to be nothing but a big and clumsy kid. George turned to baseball and pitching. There he made a much different impression. In fact, George was so good on the mound that flattering offers to enter professional baseball came to him from both the Chicago Cubs and the Pittsburgh Pirates.

But George Mikan had his heart set on a different goal. He wanted to become a priest. Feeling that basketball was still his best bet to win an education, he sought a scholarship at Notre Dame. George Keogan, at that time coach of the Notre Dame five, watched the tall youngster work out on the court and turned thumbs down. That famous court mentor thought the big fellow was too slow, too ponderous, too heavy to play basketball. So Mikan did not get into Notre Dame.

Instead, he enrolled at DePaul University in Chicago where basketball was a major sport. That was in 1943. Still foremost in his mind was his desire to become a priest. He took all the courses at that fine Catholic school which would lead him to his cherished goal. But again George struck an obstacle. It was necessary for him to master Greek to go on to what he wanted. But he could not make a go of it. Greek proved an insurmountable barrier. He turned to other studies, and began to prepare himself for the law.

Meanwhile, George played basketball. At DePaul, his big body, his great weight, his slowness of foot, were somehow not noticed, or else ignored. Even the fact that the big fellow was obliged to wear thick glasses to correct his extreme nearsightedness made no difference. The DePaul coach had George's eyes fitted with non-shattering lenses and strapped the glasses to his temples with tape. Not always did the special harness work. In one game, his glasses were broken during a hot scrimmage under the basket. Mikan strapped on a fresh pair, stayed in the game, and went on to score the points that meant victory. Afterwards, a surgeon took six stitches in his face.

George Mikan played basketball at DePaul for four years. They were phenomenal years during which the big man set all sorts of incredible scoring records. He was chosen All-American in 1944, 1945 and 1946. In two of those years he was honored as Player of the Year. And enduring fame was added when he was made a member of the All-Time All-American college basketball team!

Mikan left college a full-fledged lawyer and famous as the greatest college basketball player that had ever lived! It was natural for professional teams to go after big George. Minneapolis offered the myopic giant a small fortune to play for the Lakers. And George decided to delay his legal career to become the highest paid basketball player in the world!

What George Mikan has done in professional basketball is already history. Against the toughest competition he had ever been called on to face, George continued to create his fantastic records. He shattered every scoring mark known to the game and set a few of his own that will probably never be equaled. And along the way, he led Minneapolis to six world's championships in his first seven years with them— making the Lakers famous as the greatest professional basketball team in the world!

An incredible performer on the court is this lumbering giant with the magic touch—in the game he once was considered too big, too heavy, too clumsy and too nearsighted to play at all!

STAN MUSIAL
What-a-Man Stan

IT WAS ABOUT the year 1938 that the humble home of Lukasz Musial, a Polish immigrant steelworker in a Donora, Pennsylvania, mill, faced a serious crisis. Lukasz's son, Stanley, had decided to become a professional baseball player instead of going to college on an athletic scholarship that had been offered him. To the elder Musial, a free college education seemed to be a great prize, a chance for the boy to escape the heat and sweat and hard work of the steel mill.

But the boy insisted. He had been offered $100 a month to pitch in the minor leagues. The stern old father finally had to relent. Stan Musial went off to play minor league ball.

For several years, Stan Musial pitched in the bush leagues with little success. He was beginning to wonder whether he had not, after all, made a serious mistake by passing up the scholarship he had once been offered. Then, one afternoon, disaster overtook the obscure young lefthander. Coming in from the mound to field a bunt, he fell heavily on his pitching shoulder. When he rose from the ground, his left arm was numb, his face was twisted with pain. It was the end of Stan Musial, mediocre minor league pitcher.

But Stan was a determined youngster. Nothing would make him quit the game he loved. Early in 1941, he appeared at a St. Louis Cardinal minor league camp in Florida. The general consensus among the St. Louis officials was that Musial was through as a pitcher, that his arm was dead and useless.

82

But Branch Rickey, then head of the Cardinal organization, saw something one morning. Musial had come to the plate for batting practice and slammed out several line drives that ripped between the outfielders like bullets. Perhaps, thought the wise Mr. Rickey, Musial could be converted into an outfielder. A man who could hit like that. . . .

That night, Stan Musial was sent to Columbus, Georgia, to convert himself into an outfielder. Orders were that he was to be taught, nursed along, watched carefully. The Columbus manager followed instructions to the letter. The rest of the story is history.

As an outfielder, Stan Musial found a new life in baseball. He moved rapidly up the ladder from that day. At 21, he was in the majors with the parent club, the Cardinals. Soon it became apparent to the entire league that one of baseball's great hitters had appeared on the scene.

Over the years, Musial was chosen most valuable player in the National League three times, a record. As a batter, he led the league six times, up to the season of 1954. And one day in that season, "What-a-Man" Stan reached the apex of his glorious career as one of the greatest hitters in baseball, when he performed the unprecedented feat of hitting five home runs in one afternoon of big league baseball. He was always an extraordinary fielder, a brilliant first baseman, a player's player and a manager's delight. And his salary soared past the $80,000 per year mark as his records piled up in the books. Not bad for a ballplayer who, before he was 21, had been considered all washed up as a minor league pitcher!

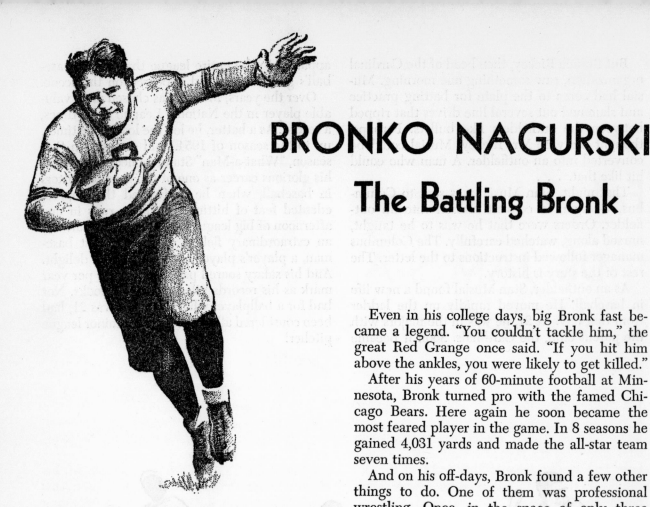

BRONKO NAGURSKI
The Battling Bronk

THE SAGA of the incomparable Bronko Nagurski began in the fall of 1926 when a husky 18-year-old from Ontario, Canada, showed up for football practice at the University of Minnesota. As a member of the freshman team, Bronko was in the line-up one day when head coach Spears brought his varsity team over to try out a new play against the freshmen. Nagurski stopped the play cold.

Spears ordered the freshmen to try the same play against the varsity, at that time one of the nation's powerhouses. The big Bronk took the ball in the frosh backfield and began to plow ahead. To the coach's wide-eyed amazement, Bronk split a hole in the vaunted varsity line as if it were made of paper!

That was the beginning. Nagurski went on to become not only Minnesota's greatest football player but the most devastating player in history. He played superlatively at any and all positions. One year, when Grantland Rice was trying to pick his All-America team, he was puzzled about where to put the great Nagurski. But one thing was certain to him: that Bronk belonged on it as the greatest football player around.

Even in his college days, big Bronk fast became a legend. "You couldn't tackle him," the great Red Grange once said. "If you hit him above the ankles, you were likely to get killed."

After his years of 60-minute football at Minnesota, Bronk turned pro with the famed Chicago Bears. Here again he soon became the most feared player in the game. In 8 seasons he gained 4,031 yards and made the all-star team seven times.

And on his off-days, Bronk found a few other things to do. One of them was professional wrestling. Once, in the space of only three weeks, he played in five tough championship football games and wrestled against eight of the best grapplers in the world. In fact, the great football star was recognized for a time as the heavyweight wrestling champion of the world!

One of the best stories about Nagurski's incredible power as a plunging fullback deals with the occasion when he got a little mad. During most of a game, Bronk had been unable to make much progress through a stubborn enemy line. Determined that he would be thwarted no longer, Bronk set himself for one last desperate plunge. Taking the ball from center, he plowed into the opposing line. He crashed through, then scattered the secondary. A moment later, big Bronk slammed into the safety man with a bang that could be heard outside the stadium. But the infuriated giant never lifted his head. Steaming ahead, he crashed into the goal post, caromed off, kept going, and then smashed head on into the thick concrete wall of the stadium.

Bronko Nagurski wobbled shakily to his feet, still clutching the football. "Man," he muttered as his teammates congratulated him on scoring the winning touchdown, "that last guy sure hit me hard!"

Father of Basketball

DR. JAMES A. NAISMITH

HE WAS BORN in a small town in Canada on a November day in 1861. And at the age of eight he became an orphan. An uncle who was a minister took over the task of raising the parentless boy. The kindly old man decided that the boy should be trained to follow in his footsteps and enter the ministry.

When the boy grew older, he was sent to McGill University to prepare himself for the pulpit. However, the youngster became interested in sports, and before he had completed his course, he had won himself a reputation as one of Canada's greatest rugby and lacrosse players.

To continue his studies, the boy came to the United States where he enrolled at the Y.M.C.A. Training School in Springfield, Massachusetts. The school was a small one in those days—there were forty students in all—but Springfield had a football team. And the boy—James Naismith —went out for the team.

Naismith was only a little fellow, as football players went in those days. He weighed a mere 160 pounds in an era when giants roamed the gridiron. Nevertheless, he made the team—and at center, no less. To make himself look as ferocious as possible, young Naismith grew a large luxuriant mustache. And to keep his ears from being torn from his head by the big vicious men he opposed in the line, he wrapped a wide band of adhesive around his head.

The young Canadian ministry student became the star of that Springfield eleven—a team that held its own against such powerhouses as Harvard and Yale. When he completed his studies, Naismith was taken to one side by his coach, a man named Amos Alonzo Stagg. Stagg convinced the young Canadian that he was more suited to spread the gospel of physical health than to become a minister. So Naismith stayed on at Springfield as an instructor of physical training.

One day, James Naismith was discussing sports with a group of friends. It was agreed that a new game was needed at Springfield, one that could be played indoors. Naismith took the problem home with him. In a few days, he had an idea. He went looking for the school janitor.

"I want a couple of square boxes," said Naismith. "Crates, if you have them."

The janitor scratched his head. "I don't have any square boxes," he replied. "But I can give you a couple of peach baskets."

Naismith accepted the peach baskets, and the rest is history. For the game that he had invented was basketball! From that beginning in 1891, basketball has come close to being the world's most popular game, with 100,000,000 people every year either playing or watching. Odd it is indeed that the only native game in the United States, a game without any foreign roots, was invented by a Canadian, James A. Naismith.

PAAVO NURMI
Phantom Finn

PAAVO NURMI began training himself to be a runner when he was still a boy. Although he had to work as a laborer from the time he was 12, Paavo managed to condition himself by chasing trolley cars through the streets of his native Abo in Finland. No day passed without some running. Never did he neglect his training. When he was inducted into the Finnish Army in 1919, the silent Finn only intensified his daily workouts. He practiced endlessly, running with a stop watch in his hand, pacing himself against record time whenever he could.

Finland sent him to the Olympics in 1920. He was beaten in his first Olympic race, the 5,000-meter event. His defeat taught him a lesson he was never to forget. It wasn't enough to run against a watch. A man had to run against his opponents, too.

In the next race, the 10,000-meter run, Nurmi captured first place. And, in 1923, Nurmi leaped into the headlines by setting a new world's record of 4:10.4 in the classic mile.

In the 1924 Olympics, Paavo Nurmi created a sensation by winning the 1,500-meter and 5,000-meter races on the same day, setting world's records in both events. Two days later, he came back to win the 10,000-meter steeplechase under a broiling sun that forced two-thirds of a big field to quit the race.

A year later, the solemn, silent Flying Finn was invited to run in the United States against the pick of the world's runners. His arrival was quiet and unheralded. In his first race, Nurmi won while breaking a world's record. The next night he ran and won again, setting another world's record. On the third night, Nurmi repeated the same procedure. In his first three nights in America, he had run three races and smashed three world's records!

And that was only the beginning. Nurmi, a stranger in an alien land, conquered the hearts of all track fans as he fashioned a tour of triumph that spanned the entire nation. One night it was New York, the next Chicago. A third night might find him another thousand miles away. Always he ran like a well-oiled machine, always he won.

In his first 24 days in the United States the incredible Finn ran races over distances that ranged from three-quarters of a mile to three miles, against the best runners in the land. During the tour, he became the first man in history to run two miles in less than nine minutes. Whatever the distance, whatever the competition, Paavo Nurmi won every race he ran in— and set the astounding total of 16 new world's records while doing so! In that memorable invasion of the United States, the Flying Finn with the stopwatch established a total of 38 different track records of one sort or another.

Perhaps some day another runner will come along to shatter so many records in so short a time. But Paavo Nurmi, who went on to win seven gold medals in three different Olympic Games, certainly deserves a permanent niche in the affections of track followers everywhere.

ANNIE OAKLEY

Little Sure Shot

BACK IN THE LAST CENTURY, a family named Mozee owned a farm just outside the city of Cincinnati. One day, someone showed a rifle to the farmer's little daughter, Annie. The child was so fascinated by the weapon that she insisted on being shown how to handle it and fire it. That was the beginning for Phoebe Ann Oakley Mozee who was to make the name Annie Oakley immortal.

By the time Annie reached her tenth birthday, she was an expert shot. And her family permitted her to go out into the fields and woods alone to shoot game.

Annie brought home so much quail that her father was able to start a thriving trade with the big provision houses in the nearby city. In no time at all, Annie was actually supporting her whole family with the proceeds from her keen marksmanship. In five short years, Annie had earned enough with her rifle to pay off the heavy mortgage on the family farm. And she had won for herself the nickname of "Little Sure Shot."

Word of the young girl's remarkable abilities with a rifle soon spread around the country. When she was barely 16, the famous scout and showman, Buffalo Bill Cody, brought his Wild West Show to Cincinnati. As soon as he arrived in town, he sent for the girl with the eagle-sharp eyes. When she appeared, he asked her to give him a demonstration of her marksmanship.

Ten minutes later, the astonished Buffalo Bill offered her a contract to travel with his troupe. Annie signed it and remained with Buffalo Bill and his show for 17 years.

Wherever she went, Annie Oakley brought crowds by the thousands to see her incredible feats with the rifle. Her unerring eye amazed all who watched her. And always they demanded to see her favorite trick—hitting pennies tossed into the air. On one special occasion, Annie gave a demonstration of this trick of hers that has never been duplicated. 5000 pennies were tossed up for her to shoot at. And she hit 4,777 of them!

She was hardly out of her teens when a marksman challenged Annie to a match. It was the first time she had ever been asked to meet a man on equal terms in a rifle-shooting contest. With her usual calm and accuracy, Annie easily defeated her male opponent. And so overcome was he by her prowess that he asked her to marry him on the spot!

In the course of her shooting exhibitions, Annie Oakley toured the entire world. It was on one of these trips that Annie was thrown into a situation that might have changed the entire course of history. Of course, Little Sure Shot did not know this at the time. But it is interesting to speculate as to what might have happened if. . . .

Annie was in Germany touring with her act when she received a summons to appear before the royal court of the Emperor himself, Kaiser Wilhelm. She performed all her best tricks for the monarch. The Kaiser was deeply impressed by Annie's skill with what he had always considered a man's weapon. When her show was over, he called her to his side.

"Could you, Fraulein, shoot a cigarette from a man's mouth at 100 paces?" he asked.

"Yes, Your Majesty," she replied.

The Kaiser smiled. "From *my* mouth?"

"Of course," replied Annie with complete confidence.

A loud murmur of horrified protest rose from the assembled court. The Kaiser must be mad to try such a foolish trick! But Wilhelm brushed them all aside. With stately dignity, he stepped off 100 paces from where Annie stood with her rifle. Then, standing in profile to the American girl, he lighted a cigarette and waited.

Annie Oakley raised her rifle to her shoulder and aimed with steady hands at the cigarette between the Kaiser's lips. Around the brilliantly illuminated salon, all heads were averted, all eyes closed to shut out the sight of the terrible thing that was going to happen. For a moment, there was deathlike silence. Then a shot rang out.

Annie was firing her rifle at the man who was, years later, to start World War I, one of Europe's bloodiest conflicts. Would history have been changed if Annie had struck the Kaiser that day? No one will know—for Annie's shot snapped the cigarette right out of the Kaiser's mouth without touching so much as a hair of his turned-up mustache!

In all the history of rifle marksmanship, there has never been so keen an eye, so accurate a shot, as the fabulous Annie Oakley! So famous has she remained through the years, that in one form or another, the stage and the motion pictures have told and retold her story. Her fame as a "sure shot" was so great that Annie Oakley became part of the American language. Because for many years during her life and for many years after her death, in show business and the sports world, a free ticket always was punched with three small holes, and always it was called an "Annie Oakley" in honor of that amazing lady who once was known to all the world as Little Sure Shot—Annie Oakley!

Mighty Muscle Man

PARRY O'BRIEN

FOR A LONG TIME, track and field history nursed three myths of the unattainable in human physical effort. They were the 15-foot pole vault, the 4-minute mile and the 60-foot shotput.

First to fall to man's refusal to accept anything as impossible was the pole-vault limit, broken by Cornelius Warmerdam. Second to go was the 4-minute mile to Roger Bannister in May, 1954.

And then, only two days after Bannister's historic mile run, the third myth of track and field was smashed by a husky 22-year-old named Parry O'Brien. O'Brien added another impossible chapter to human endeavor by tossing the 16-pound shot a distance of 60 feet, 5¼ inches.

Parry O'Brien, first man to throw the shot over 60 feet, was not reared to be a shot-putter. His father had been a record-breaking football star at Santa Monica High School in California, as well as a professional ballplayer with ten years in the minors and a short stay with the Philadelphia Athletics. Thus young Parry grew

up in an atmosphere of athletic accomplishment. The senior O'Brien, wanting his boy to follow in his footsteps as a football star, drilled young Parry from boyhood on.

Unhappily, Parry was only a slight 145-pounder when the time came for him go to Santa Monica High. It looked as if he would never play any sport, least of all football. Then, miraculously and practically overnight, he shot up to 6 feet and 200 pounds. He became a clever, rugged football star at the high school. And, just as his father had hoped, he won a football scholarship to the University of Southern California.

But he never became a college football luminary. A strange ambition had suddenly come to him. He became obsessed with the idea of becoming a great shot-putter. It got so bad that he filled the family garage with all sorts of weight-lifting gadgets to build up his strength, and he stayed up nights reading books and articles on the art of shot-putting. He even practiced heaving the iron ball late at night in a vacant lot by the light of a lone street lamp. And often, in the privacy of his room, he practiced before a mirror.

As can be imagined, O'Brien, senior, was not enthusiastic about his son's new and absorbing interest. Nor did the football coaches at USC think any more of what the lad was up to. But no one could discourage the youngster. Convinced that the form employed by the great weight men of the past was outdated, he began to experiment with a strange new style of his own. It horrified the track coaches who saw it. But after 5 years of constant practice and some 40,000 practice throws, it paid off. First, Parry O'Brien broke the world's record. Then, in the Olympic Games of 1952, he hurled the 16-pound ball 57 feet, 1½ inches, 11 inches further than the previous Olympic mark. As he neared the magic figure of 60 feet, Parry worked harder and harder with no other thought in mind than to reach that mark, and be the first man in history to do so.

The historic moment came on May 8, 1954. The startled world barely had time to recover from this shattering of an ancient myth when big Parry calmly went out and did it again—and yet again, breaking the 60-foot mark four times within the month and pushing his incredible record to a fantastic 60 feet, 10 inches. The old myth, stubborn though it had been, was dead. Parry O'Brien, newly crowned immortal, took its place in the pages of sports history.

BARNEY OLDFIELD

America's First Speed Demon

BARNEY OLDFIELD was the first man ever to drive an automobile a mile a minute. In spite of the terrible hazards of speed racing in the early days of the automobile, Barney Oldfield, his familiar cigar clenched between his teeth, spent fifteen frenzied years behind the wheel of his racing cars. There were few safety devices in those days. Blowouts were frequent, and mechanical failures brought death to many a driver. But through it all, Barney Oldfield roared along, making the automobile familiar to a world of excited fans.

Thanks to him, the new-fangled automobile soon caught on with the public. After watching Oldfield's exploits on the dirt tracks, everybody wanted to ride in a horseless carriage!

Barney Oldfield became the daredevil of the roads in a curious way. Shortly after the turn of the century he was working as a helper to a racing driver-mechanic who owned his own car and who was getting it ready for an important road race.

Things went well until the early morning of the race. Oldfield's boss took the car out for a short run. He climbed out of the vehicle, a look of disgust on his oil-smeared face.

"I'm sick of these things breaking down," he said to Oldfield. "I'm quitting racing. I'll sell you this car for $200."

"I'll take it," said Oldfield, who had never driven a car.

Oldfield looked the car over, saw it was in good working order, and then went looking for a driver to take the place of the man who had sold it to him.

But there was no longer a driver available for the race. There was only one thing for him to do—and Barney Oldfield did it. He got behind the wheel of his newly purchased racing car and taught himself to drive.

A couple of hours later, Barney Oldfield took that racing car, his first speed wagon, out on the dirt road. And he won the race from the best racing drivers in the country. The car that Barney Oldfield drove was to become famous all over the world as "999." And the man who sold it to him was Henry Ford.

Barney Oldfield became America's speed king. As the years passed, Oldfield and his cigar roared to one triumph after another. There were crashes now and then, but always his luck held. He lived on to become a national institution, his famous racers a part of the language and his own name a synonym for speed.

FRANCIS OUIMET
He Gave Golf to the People

GOLF is played today by many millions of Americans who, years ago, would never have dreamed of taking part in a game which was once the hobby of the rich and aristocratic. It was no accident that the sport of golf was opened to all. One man was largely responsible —and he was Francis Ouimet.

It was back in 1913 that Francis Ouimet, an obscure young ex-caddy of 19, created the great golf drama that has since become a legend of that ancient game. England then was the golfing center of the world. In America, golf was the exclusive province of an idle handful of socialites who found it an amusing plaything for their declining years.

The American Open Golf championship of 1913 was held at Brookline in Massachusetts, and England, as a gesture of courtesy, sent her two greatest golfers, Harry Vardon and Ted Ray, to participate in the event. It was a foregone conclusion that one of the Britons would easily walk off with the crown. For Vardon was the symbol of all that was perfect in golf, and Ted Ray was the mightiest hitter in the game, a genius of the links.

One of the entrants in the Open was Francis Ouimet, a store clerk. Little was expected from that obscure young man. All eyes were on Vardon and Ray, the greatest players of their time.

With only one round left to play, there was sensational news. The young amateur, Ouimet, had come off the links tied for the lead with the two British titans. A few expressed their gratification that an American had done so well so far. Of course, the Englishmen would put a stop to the nonsense in the final round and win as they pleased. Nevertheless, it was thrilling that an unknown teen-ager was giving the two most famous golfers in the world such a dramatic battle for top honors. Of course, such a miracle couldn't last.

But it did last. Out of the slanting rain beating down on the Brookline golf course that day, came the amazing Ouimet and he finished that championship golf tournament in a flat tie with the two most famous golfers England ever had. And now all three—Vardon, Ray and Ouimet— were forced into a play-off for the title.

Despite his superb finish, this time everyone was sure that the 19-year-old boy from Boston would crack under the pressure and that the title would pass to either Vardon or Ray. But with the odds against him, Francis Ouimet stuck to his grim task. Again, single-handed, he repulsed the attack of the British invaders. Rising to superb heights, Ouimet polished off an amazing round of championship golf that saw him finish five strokes ahead of Harry Vardon and six in front of Ted Ray.

The dramatic feat of Francis Ouimet electrified the nation. The headlines hailed his feat as the most stimulating single event the game has ever known. That moment marked the beginning of golf as a popular sport in America. Following Ouimet's great victory, people from all walks of life began to play the game. Now, more than twenty million people play golf, and it all really came to happen because one day a 19-year-old boy created the glorious golf legend of: "Ouimet Wins at Brookline!"

JESSE OWENS
America's Answer

IT WAS on a sunny afternoon in May, 1935, that Jesse Owens, an obscure student at Ohio State University, burst like a meteor on a startled sports world. Competing in a Big Ten track meet at Ann Arbor, the 20-year-old Negro boy from an Alabama cotton-picker's shack who had been forced to work ever since he was six, ran and jumped to victory in four events in a single afternoon. In winning those events, he broke three world's records and tied a fourth.

To begin with, Jesse tied a world's record while winning the 100-yard dash. He followed by setting new world marks for the 220-yard dash and the 220-yard low hurdles. And he closed out his great day leaping for the longest broad jump ever made by man, 26 feet, 8¼ inches—a world's record that still stands. No greater one-man performance had ever before been seen in track and field!

It was the beginning of the glorious saga of one of America's all-time track greats. By the time the trials for the 1936 Olympic Games came around, Jesse was being called the world's fastest human. Qualified for all his favorite events, he sailed with the United States Olympic squad to Berlin, Germany, for that international carnival.

In 1936, Adolf Hitler was near the crest of his terrifying power as the world's most feared man. He ruled Nazi Germany with an iron fist. He boasted that the Olympic Games would prove that German athletes were the fastest and strongest—the supermen of the world. Jesse Owens, the 21-year-old humble American boy shattered Hitler's boasts of Aryan supermen and focused the scorn of the world on the Nazi race theories.

On the first day of the games, two Germans won gold medals and were warmly congratulated by the beaming dictator himself in his royal box. Next day, Owens blazed to victory in the 100-meter dash as he covered that distance in 10.3 to set an Olympic and world record. But Hitler refused to receive him in his box and shake his hand.

On the third day of the Olympic Games, Jesse was entered in the running broad jump. The greatest in the world were to compete against him, including the mighty Lutz Long, the German champion.

To warm up for the event, Owens jogged down the chute to the jump-off place, and over-ran the take-off line. To his consternation, the officials charged the practice leap as one of his regular jumps. But Jesse did not protest. He went back to the starting line, thundered down the runway and took off in a magnificent leap. But the officials did not even bother to measure the jump. The loudspeakers blared forth with the announcement that the American had committed a foul.

Now Jesse was left with but one more jump to top Lutz Long, the German entry, who was leading the field. He had to make sure there would be no question about the fairness of his jump, nor a doubt that he had committed a foul by overstepping the take-off line. So before going back to jump again, Jesse Owens leaned down and drew a line of his own, one foot behind the official take-off line.

The huge crowd in that vast Olympic Stadium froze into a breathless silence as the lean glistening ebony body of Jesse Owens hurdled down the runway and took off into space, his legs sawing for distance. Soon came the official announcement. Owens had set an Olympic record for the broad jump—26 feet, 5 5/16 inches. It still stands.

But again an embarrassed Adolf Hitler refused to receive the American Negro star, and shake his hand in token of victory. And when, on the following day, Owens won the 200-meter dash in 20.3 seconds to set another Olympic record, Hitler was so flustered that he actually ducked out of his royal box and fled from the stadium to avoid having to congratulate the amazing American.

With three Olympic records and three gold medals already stowed away, Jesse Owens was not yet done with his fantastic Olympic victory. He went out and won a fourth gold medal as a member of the United States' 400-meter relay team which set an Olympic and world record of 39.8. No greater one-man performance had ever before been seen in Olympic Games history.

After his Olympic triumphs, Jesse continued running until he was almost 35. He raced in England, France, Italy, Norway, Spain, Portugal and North Africa. Only when he no longer could run the 100 yards in faster time than 9.7 seconds, he gave up foot racing.

In 1951 Owens returned to Germany for a visit. Adolf Hitler was dead and Nazi Germany had been destroyed in a bloody World War. He made an appearance at the Olympic stadium where he had scored his magnificent triumphs in 1936. Seventy-five thousand people were there to greet him. This time there was no arrogant dictator to snub him, for in the official box sat the Mayor of Berlin. And when Owens dressed in his old Olympic track outfit slowly raced around the track to the wild cheers of the crowd, and then jogged over to the box, the Mayor rose and held out his arms.

"Fifteen years ago Hitler would not shake your hand," he said. "Here, I give you both of mine." And he threw his arms around Jesse's neck and hugged him.

Jesse Owens' reward for what he had accomplished in the Olympic Games had been a long time coming. But come it did, at last to close the saga of glory for an all-time track great.

The Golden Boy of the Cinder Track

CHARLES PADDOCK

ONE OF THOSE who helped create America's golden age of sports in the 1920's was Charley Paddock, the man who came to be known in his time as the world's fastest human. A blond and husky Texan who ran in the colors of the University of Southern California, Paddock was the most glamorous figure ever developed in American track history. Almost unbeaten as a dash man, he set no less than 95 sprint records.

In the 1920 Olympics, Charley Paddock blazed to victory in the 100-meter dash. A year later, he set a world record of 9.6 for 100 yards and, a little later the same day, sped 220 yards in 21.8 seconds. In the same year, the golden boy set a mark for the 300-meter run that stands to this day.

There was a lot about Charley Paddock that was refreshingly different. To begin with, he came to U.S.C. with a reputation as a poet and playwright. Before earning renown as a sprinter, one of his plays was produced in a Los Angeles theatre. But most of all, Charley fairly glowed with color. The big, tow-headed speedster was a man with personality plus.

As a runner, he broke all the established rules of sprinting. He did everything wrong—except finish ahead of the field. And he was oddly superstitious. Fond of wearing a baby-blue track suit and white running shoes, he went through a ritual of knocking on wood and fussing over his starting holes before a race. He was a bundle of nerves, jittery, anxious to be off. But when the gun exploded, Paddock exploded with it like a flaming rocket. At the finish there was his celebrated jump to bring the fans to their feet in a buzz of excitement. For Charley Paddock could not just run to the tape like any other sprinter. He had to soar through the air over the last 18 feet or so to finish like a bird in flight.

Three times Charley Paddock represented the United States in the Olympic games, in 1920, 1924 and 1928. Always he charmed everyone around him with his wit and gaiety.

Like the true champion he was, Charley Paddock quickly joined the colors when World War II started. Although past 40, he soon became Captain Paddock of the United States Marine Corps. In this new role, America's most glamorous runner finally met his match—the Old Man with the stopwatch that nobody beats. He died a hero high above the Alaska ice in a blazing Navy plane.

Millions who had seen him run mourned for the man once called the world's fastest human. Many millions more, to whom Charley Paddock was a symbol of America's most colorful era in sports, also grieved at the loss of one of the most irrepressible runners of our times.

LESTER PATRICK
An Old Man in the Net

MAN AND BOY, Lester Patrick spent more than forty years in big-time hockey, as player, manager, coach and owner. No more amazing career has been fashioned in this Canadian-born game than by the man who has been called simply "Mr. Hockey."

Himself a Canadian, Patrick turned naturally to playing hockey as a youngster. In his teens he was generally acclaimed as the greatest amateur hockey player in the world. And when he turned professional with the fabulous Renfrew Millionaires, he began a career of 19 years as a major league hockey star.

What he accomplished as a player is a matter of history. He revolutionized the game, won fame as the greatest defenseman of them all, sparked teams to world championships in Stanley Cup competition. As a player and manager, Patrick figured in over 20 such Stanley Cup victories. But whatever he did as a player or as a manager must pale in significance when compared to a single episode in his life that has since become a shining legend of the game.

It was a night in March, 1928. The New York Rangers, managed by old, silver-thatched Lester Patrick, were playing the powerful Montreal Maroons for the Stanley Cup, symbol of the world's professional hockey championship.

During the second game of the series, a flying puck caromed off a hockey stick and struck Lorne Chabot, New York's goalie, square in the eye. Chabot dropped like a felled ox, his hands clapped to his bleeding face. So agonizing was the pain he suffered that he soon lost consciousness. Supine and motionless, the Ranger goalie lay sprawled on the ice before his net.

In the arena, 12,000 fans, who had been roaring with excitement only a moment before, now sat hushed and silent. Quickly a stretcher was brought out on the ice and the stricken goalie was carried off to the hospital. Meanwhile the desperate and stunned Rangers huddled around their manager, Lester Patrick.

A moment later, the referee of the game joined them. "Let's get going!" he ordered sharply. "Put another goalie out on the ice!"

96

"We don't have another goalie," groaned Patrick. And he looked around at his squad. Someone would have to go into the nets, the game had to go on. Defense men and forwards he had plenty. Which one of them could he put in to replace the injured Chabot?

Not one of his spares had experience as a goalie, and goal-tending, as he well knew, was an art in itself. The Maroons, as tough and aggressive a team as could be found anywhere, would like nothing better than to have a green and inexperienced goal-tender in the nets. They would take the poor fellow apart in a matter of seconds. No, thought Lester Patrick, that would be a cruel thing to do to any one of his boys. If somebody had to be sacrificed, it would have to be. . . .

So manager Lester Patrick, a man approaching fifty years of age, climbed into a Ranger uniform himself, drew on a pair of goalie shin pads, and skated uncertainly out on the ice. He had not played in years, had not even worn skates for a long time. Now he found himself in the Ranger nets prepared to play in a Stanley Cup championship game against the roughest crew in hockey! In the stands, the fans buzzed with anticipation of the slaughter, and on the ice, the Maroons got ready to give old Lester Patrick the worst time of his life.

The heroic stand made by rusty, old Lester Patrick that night was the most astounding sight any sport has ever presented. Blinded by perspiration, wobbly and weary on his skates, the old gentleman stood to his guns in the Ranger nets and forced his aching and protesting muscles to do his bidding. Time and again, the Maroons swooped down on the old man, flinging themselves at him in waves as they attempted to score. Each time he made incredible stops, repulsed every power play that came his way.

The Rangers had gone on the ice expecting to see their white-haired coach cut to pieces in the nets. Now they took fire from the example the old man was setting. They forgot everything except that their leader was giving his all for them.

From the very jaws of defeat, the New York Rangers, playing like so many men possessed, snatched the prize they had almost given up hope of winning when their regular goalie had been injured. With their gallant leader playing like a fiend behind them, they went on to win, not only that game, but also the series and the most prized trophy in all the world of hockey, the Stanley Cup!

Lester Patrick has achieved fame in hockey for many reasons. As a player and coach, he stands out as the greatest of them all. He has even given two sons to the game who have followed worthily in his footsteps as players and coaches of major-league hockey teams. But never did Lester Patrick do anything which more richly deserved to be called great than that inspiring night when, as an old and long-since retired player, he went into the nets as goalie to lead his New York Rangers to victory and a world's championship!

The Little Knight on a Racehorse

GORDON RICHARDS

WHEN A MAN becomes a champion in his particular sport, and remains at the top of the field for several years, it is a noteworthy achievement. If he can hold his title for a decade, he is an outstanding figure in the world of sports. But when a man can be a champion for over a quarter of a century, it is almost a certainty that one is in the presence of true sports greatness.

Gordon Richards, tiny king of all the jockeys, brought his 1953 season to a triumphant close when he took top honors among English jockeys by riding more winners than any other rider. With 191 winners to his credit, the old master had won the English riding championship for the 26th time! In 31 years of riding, Gordon Richards had failed to be the top jockey in Great Britain only five times! And the total number of winners ridden by Gordon Richards had reached the fantastic figure of nearly 5,000!

To be a champion for over a quarter of a century is an amazing feat even for as great a rider as Gordon Richards has been for so many years.

The little man—he is not quite five feet tall and weighs barely 110 pounds—has through the years amazed the followers of the turf by his skill and daring in the saddle. And yet, there is an even more fantastic story in the life of England's and the world's greatest jockey of modern times.

Shortly after the turn of the century, a son was born to a six-dollar-a-week coal miner in a village in Shropshire near the Wales border. The boy was named Gordon by his father, and his future seemed certain to be like that of every other boy in the village. Gordon would some day himself be a miner in the coal pits.

Poverty was the lot of young Gordon, as it was of his playmates in the village. Until he was 14 years of age, he never owned a piece of clothing that had been bought for him. Everything he wore had been made for him at home or handed down from his elders. And all the money he had ever had was the couple of pennies a week he sometimes got as an allowance.

Gordon lived in this grinding misery until he was 14—and then he rebelled. He rebelled against hunger and hand-me-down rags and, more than anything else, he rebelled against the future that loomed before him. Soon he would be called on to go down into the pits of the mine, into the darkness and the cold and the filth that he would never leave again as long as he lived.

With such a fate staring him in the face, Gordon took the first opportunity that offered and ran away from home. Soon he had found himself what was practically a gentleman's job. He was hired as an office boy at the magnificent salary of about a dollar a week!

One day, after having worked as an office boy for about a year, Gordon read an advertisement in a paper for a stable apprentice. He had never grown very much, and it seemed to the Shropshire lad that he might make good use of his tiny size around horses. True, he knew nothing about them. But he could try. And then, there might be more money to be earned than a dollar a week.

Gordon applied for the job and got it—and at double the salary he had been receiving! Happy, and fired with new ambition, he worked hard and listened to everything he was told. And he learned fast, so fast that he was soon being allowed to ride.

Two years later, Gordon Richards rode his first winner as a jockey. And a fantastic saga of the turf had begun!

Before he turned 21, Gordon became the champion jockey of England. And over the years that followed, he won the top honors again and again. Along the way, many records fell to Richards. None was more striking than the winning streak he ran up in 1933. That year he set a world's record for riding successive winners when, over a period of three days, he booted home 12 in a row!

It is no wonder that Gordon Richards became a national celebrity in a land that so loves horse racing. The once poor son of an obscure coal miner in Shropshire came to be the friend of England's great—leaders in finance, industry and the arts.

And he himself became one of the wealthiest men in Britain. His nearly 5,000 winners in over 20,000 mounts brought him more than $3,000,-000 in earnings. Although crowding the half-century mark in age, Gordon Richards was still adding to his earnings and winning record when most men were willing to lean back and enjoy a well-earned rest.

Among his many friends, Gordon Richards also counted many members of the royal family. And in 1953, there came to him the highest honor ever bestowed on a jockey anywhere in the world. For Gordon Richards, the Shropshire coal miner's son who had soared to the very top of the heap as Britain's greatest jockey was knighted by Queen Elizabeth for his achievements. To all his other honors, he added the new title—Sir Gordon Richards! Sir Gordon Richards—only jockey in modern times to be made a knight!

MAURICE RICHARD

The Rocket of the Ice

IN 1936, the famed Montreal Canadiens of the National Hockey League received a request which most professional clubs are accustomed to get at one time or another. Jacques Fontaine, the 14-year-old manager of a kid's hockey team in the outlying slum area of Montreal, appealed to the Canadiens for money to help outfit the club with hockey equipment.

There is always a lot of worn and surplus equipment in the possession of a big pro outfit, and the Canadiens were more than glad to oblige the youngster. But the response to the gift was not so usual. The grateful Fontaine wrote back to the club after receiving the generous present.

"Thanks a million," he wrote. "We won't ever forget what you've done for us. In five years I promise to pay you back by sending you a real good hockey player."

The Montreal management just smiled over the letter and filed it away. They were perfectly satisfied with the good deed they had done, and never expected anything to come of the kid's promise.

In 1941—five years later—a tall, frail-looking young man of 20 knocked on the door of the Montreal office. "I'm Maurice Richard," he said shyly. "Jacques Fontaine sent me."

"What for?" asked the Canadiens' manager.

"To play hockey," answered Richard simply.

After a while, the promise that had been made five years before was recalled in the Canadiens' office. Tickled by the whole idea, the manager decided to give the unlikely-looking Richard a tryout. And hockey history was on the way to being made.

For Maurice Richard turned out to be not just a good hockey player, but the best puck-chaser that had ever played the game. The greatest shot in hockey, Richard established and smashed record after record. In spite of many injuries early in his career—he broke a wrist and both ankles before he had been playing very long—Richard got better and better as time went on. By 1944, he was the most feared player in the game. Not only was his shot the hardest and most deceptive in ice hockey, but his temper was so explosive and his left hook when enraged so potent, that he became the man to watch in every game he played. Often two men were put on him to hold his scoring down, but nothing could ever control him completely.

It was in 1944 that Maurice Richard smashed the all-time record for a season's goals by driving 50 shots into the nets. By 1952, he was approaching the record of most goals scored in a lifetime. And when he finally scored his 325th goal, thereby setting a new National Hockey League record for scoring, the puck with which the new mark was set was withdrawn from the

contest, Maurice Richard's portrait was engraved on it, and it was then sent as a memento of the historic occasion to Queen Elizabeth of England.

Every time thereafter that Richard scored another goal, he merely pushed his own phenomenal record that much higher. And every time he fired that high-powered shot, measured by the electric eye at 80 miles an hour, the silent, black-haired, trigger-tempered Maurice Richard won ever more acclaim as the greatest ice-hockey player in the game.

TEX RICKARD
Greatest of Boxing Promoters

HE CAME FROM the rolling plains of far-off Texas, and his favorite expression was, "I never seed anything like it." But he saw more things on the face of this earth than most people ever get to see. Tex Rickard, greatest of boxing promoters, was always a restless man. Seeking gold and fame wherever he could find them, he wandered the frozen wastes of the Yukon territory. He won and lost a fortune in the fabled Klondike, went on to work as a cowhand in South America, and as a feared, gun-toting marshal in the western bad lands. Wherever he roamed, Tex Rickard followed his rainbow, seeking always the pot of gold that lay at its end.

Eventually, the wanderer from Texas came to the boom town of Goldfield, Nevada. There he established a dance hall with gambling on the side where a man with a poke could slake his thirst or have a crack at the games of fortune.

At the time, the peerless Joe Gans was world's lightweight champion, and the redoubtable Battling Nelson was his bitterest challenger for the crown. No promoter was able to get the two men into the ring.

But Tex Rickard did—and did it by bringing them together practically in the middle of the desert. Boldly he offered a purse of $30,000—a record for those days. And to show the whole world that he meant business, Rickard put the $30,000 pile of silver dollars in a store window for all to see!

With this beginning, Tex Rickard was on his way. He staged the Jim Jeffries–Jack Johnson fight for the heavyweight title and, with a pistol strapped to his waist, refereed the historic contest himself. Other big fights followed. And at last Rickard reached a goal as a promoter that had never before been approached. He staged the first million-dollar fight in all boxing history when he brought together Jack Dempsey and Georges Carpentier in the so-called "battle of the century" before 80,000 fans paying more than a million and three-quarter dollars to attend!

Not once, but five times did Tex Rickard promote matches with gates of over a million dollars. Never did boxing flourish as it did under the daring and imaginative direction of this former wanderer from Texas. Madison Square Garden in New York, most famous of boxing arenas, stands as a memorial to the man who was the greatest boxing promoter in history! For it is called, even to this day, "The House That Tex Built!"

EDDIE RICKENBACKER

The Ace of Aces

EVEN HAD Eddie Rickenbacker not become a hero in war, he would have remained a sports hero as one of the greatest racing drivers of all time. His career, rich in incident and accomplishment, began humbly enough with a poor boyhood in Columbus, Ohio. His first job came when he was but 15 years of age. He was paid six dollars a week to carve names on tombstones.

It didn't look like a place with a future to young Eddie, and he gave it up for another job paying only four dollars a week. This time he found himself working in a garage. And, as he tinkered with that new and exciting form of transportation known as the automobile, Eddie felt the cut in pay was well worth it.

For several years, he served as an apprentice around the auto-racing tracks. Then one day—before Eddie had turned twenty—he entered his first race.

It was no easy contest that Rickenbacker chose for his debut in the world of racing. Against him in a tough 100-mile race over a dirt track was the great speed demon, Barney Old-field. No one gave the young driver much of a chance to win—but he did.

After that first race, Eddie Rickenbacker went on to become the greatest of the racing drivers. As the recognized speed king of the world, he won many sensational automobile races. And then along came World War I. Eddie went into uniform—as a chauffeur.

It was a great honor for Eddie to become General Pershing's own private driver in France. But Eddie felt cramped, He wanted action. He appealed to the general. And Pershing released him to the air corps.

Rickenbacker learned to fly in seventeen lessons. He quickly became the ace among aces. By the end of the war he had brought down 21 German planes and fired four observation balloons. When he returned to America, he was no longer just a famous automobile driver. He was a national hero.

In the years that followed, Eddie Rickenbacker became more famous than ever. His life was one of constant adventure. He defied death again and again, always to escape. Just prior to World War II, he was in a terrible plane crash, but recovered after weeks near death.

When the second world war came, Eddie again went in search of adventure. Already head of a great airline, he became adviser to the Secretary of War. One day, an important secret mission took him flying over the vast Pacific Ocean. When his plane caught fire and plummeted into the sea, all hope was abandoned for the great sports hero and flyer. But after an incredible saga of suffering in a small rubber raft, drifting helplessly on the open sea for many days, Rickenbacker again foiled his adversary, death. He came back to prove himself as always, a living symbol of courage, a hero who could lick death in war as well as in sports!

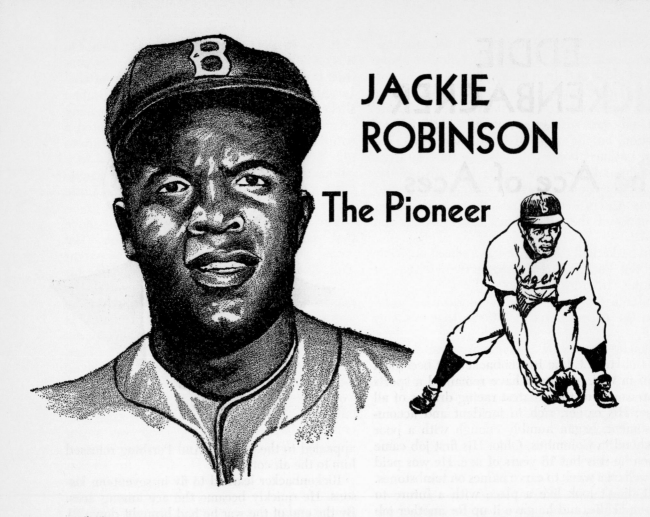

JACKIE
ROBINSON

The Pioneer

EVERY SPRING there are literally dozens of new young players who come into the major leagues, and all are watched closely to see whether there is among them another Musial or DiMaggio, Ruth or Wagner. The year 1947 was no exception. The usual crop of brilliant youngsters were up for the first time. But all eyes were on one ballplayer, and one alone, that year. He was a 28-year-old playing at first base for the Brooklyn Dodgers. They watched him because he was blazing a new trail in baseball history. He was Jackie Robinson, the first Negro player in the major leagues.

Through the years since that first appearance on the national baseball scene, the spotlight never wavered. The eyes of baseball fans still sought out the familiar figure of Jackie Robinson on the playing field. But it was no longer because, as a Negro, he was breaking new ground in baseball. It was rather because fans always watch an authentic star as he goes about his business. For that is what Jackie Robinson became. He started as an experiment in social living. He ended as a truly great baseball player,

one entitled to stand shoulder to shoulder with the immortals of the game.

Born Jack Roosevelt Robinson on January 31, 1917, in Cairo, Georgia, little Jackie was brought by his widowed mother to Pasadena, California, as a small boy. Jackie had three brothers and a sister, and life was hard for all of them. Jackie shined shoes, sold scrap metal, hawked hot dogs at the Rose Bowl, to help support the family.

Jackie was always playing games with the other kids, and when he entered high school at Pasadena, he quickly became a star in four major sports: football, basketball, track and baseball. Oddly enough, he liked baseball least of all the games he played. He followed an older brother to Pasadena Junior College, and there broke that brother's broad jump record with his own leap of 25 feet, 6½ inches. And, of course, he continued to star at basketball and baseball.

The prowess of this young Negro athlete attracted the attention of the big West Coast universities and soon Jackie was offered—and accepted—an athletic scholarship at UCLA. There he continued to shine in sports. It was the happiest period in his life, and his fellow-students grew to love and even idolize him. As a gridiron great, Jackie's speed and skill as a ball-carrier made him a standout on the football field. He not only ran with phenomenal speed and deception, but he could also pass and block. He won national honors in 1938 as the country's best ground-gainer, averaging 12 yards per try. He led the country's best in yardage of returned punts. And in 1940 and 1941, his name appeared in many of the All-America rosters across the land.

In basketball too, Jackie was a sensation, leading the Pacific Coast League two seasons in scoring. In track, he broke the Pacific Coast Conference running broad jump record. And he won the national college title in that event as well.

Jackie was a whiz at any sport, probably the best all-around athlete in the land. He played topflight tennis, golf in the low 80's, boxed with professional skill. And, though it seems like an afterthought, he played shortstop on the UCLA baseball team.

A fatal accident that took his brother's life forced Jackie to leave school in his junior year in order to earn a living. When World War II broke out, he went into the service, coming out a second lieutenant. For a year he coached the basketball team at Sam Houston College in Texas, winning the city championship with his boys. But an offer to play baseball with the Kansas City Monarchs came along. The temptation of $400 a month was too great. Jackie went off to play baseball.

It was in 1945 that the big break came. On August 29th of that year, Jackie signed a contract to play with Montreal of the International League, a Brooklyn farm club. It was Branch Rickey, boss at the time of Brooklyn's far-flung organization, who took the step that created a nationwide sensation. Robbie, the first Negro to play in organized ball, sparked Montreal to a pennant in 1946. For himself he won the league batting crown and starred in winning the Little World Series.

The following spring, Rickey made the move that really shook baseball to its heels. The young Negro star was brought up to the parent club. Robbie's task in breaking ground for his race in major league ball was monumental. His personal anguish, the insults and humiliation he had to bear, are all a part of history. Robbie bore with the hard riding like the real sportsman he is. He won honors as Rookie of the Year. The league accepted him as a solid player. Other Negroes began to appear in both leagues. Robbie himself went on to become one of baseball's top players. He worked at first base, second, third, and the outfield, and was a star wherever he was put. He won the National League batting crown. He shone in All-Star games and was a prime factor in helping the Brooklyn club win four league pennants from 1947 through 1953.

Now baseball has many great Negro players, and both fans and players take them in stride. But it must never be forgotten that it was Jackie Robinson, first Negro to enter the major leagues, who led the way!

RAY ROBINSON

Sugar Ray

"HE'S A SWEET fighter—sweet as sugar!"

That's what the boxing fans thought of Ray Robinson as a fighting man and that is why they called him Sugar Ray Robinson.

The story of Sugar Ray Robinson is essentially the tale of an unhappy, lonely and ragged urchin who used to dance in Harlem streets for the pennies that meant the difference between a little hunger and downright starvation. Often enough, the boy had to fight the bigger fellows who tried to grab his pennies. In doing so, he learned how to handle himself. One thing led to another. He started boxing as an amateur. Although his real name was Walker Smith, he assumed the ring name of Robinson because Bill Robinson, world-famous tap-dancer, was his idol.

As an amateur boxer, Sugar Ray ran up a phenomenal record. He participated in 90 bouts and made a clean sweep of them all. Then, in 1939, he won the Golden Gloves title as a featherweight and was ready to turn pro. Three years later, he won the welterweight championship of

the world. He never lost it in the ring. When his 147-pound division ran out of challengers, Ray sought new worlds to conquer. He went after the middleweight crown, and won that, too.

In eleven years of boxing, Ray Robinson never suffered the ignominy of a knockout. One of the most poignant events of his career came when he attempted to win the light heavyweight crown. On a hot summer's night, he was leading by a good margin after 13 rounds when the 104-degree temperature in the ring caused him to collapse in his corner before the next round could start.

Ray Robinson retired as the undefeated middleweight champion of the world. In the opinion of experts, he was pound for pound and inch for inch the greatest fighter of his era.

As a fighter, he had earned the reputation of being cold, hard and mean. In the ring he fought viciously, asking no quarter and giving none. Once, when a man he fought died after the bout, he was asked: "Did you notice at any time whether your opponent was in trouble?" Robinson replied coldly, "Getting people in trouble is my business."

By the time he was ready to retire, Ray had amassed a fortune, both in the ring and outside. He had also begun to show a new side to his nature. One of his last fights saw him contribute all but one dollar of his sizable purse to a cancer fund. People were amazed at this seeming generosity on the part of a man considered the hardest and shrewdest bargainer in boxing. Then the reason came out. When Ray was a boy

he had one close friend who also wanted to be a fighter. But the friend made little progress in the ring. And one day cancer struck him down. Sugar Ray took care of his friend to his dying day. And when he lost his pal, Sugar Ray resolved to help others fight the dread disease that had struck down his friend. The purse he gave away was the first installment on the resolution he had made.

Strangely enough, after Ray Robinson retired from the ring, he became a dancer and a stage entertainer, so popular that he was paid as much as $15,000 a week to perform.

The Bald Eagle

KNUTE ROCKNE

ON MARCH 31, 1931, an airplane crash in a Kansas cornfield snuffed out the life of a 43-year-old passenger named Knute Rockne. The accident brought to an abrupt close one of the most colorful and successful careers in football history. The death of the bald, broken-nosed Rockne dismayed all lovers of football. At Notre Dame, where he had for 13 years led some of the most magnificent teams in the land, Rockne's loss was irreparable. Elsewhere, the man with a million friends left nothing but mourners. For Knute Rockne was a master of gridiron strategy, an inspiring teacher, a wise leader. A genius died in that crash over Kansas, but he left an impression on football that is evident to this day.

Knute Rockne was the son of a Norwegian carriage maker who brought his small boy to this country at the age of five. Young Knute worked hard as a youngster. At high school he played football and dreamed of some day being a chemist. He saved a little money working during the summers. And when the time came for him to go to college he chose Notre Dame because the tuition there was low. At the time, Notre Dame was little known outside of South Bend, Indiana.

At Notre Dame, Rockne went out for track and then switched to football. He played first at halfback, then at end. As an end, Rockne was the guiding figure in the shocking defeat that Notre Dame handed to a powerful Army team in 1913. Together with his close friend and roommate, Gus Dorais, Rockne had worked out the first modern use of the forward pass as a weapon of attack—and with it, overnight, he put Notre Dame on the national map as a great football power.

After his graduation in 1914, Rockne taught chemistry and helped coach. In 1917, he was appointed head coach of the Notre Dame football team and began the magic thirteen years of imaginative and daring leadership that was to make his name a byword across the land. Prematurely bald, he became famed as the Bald Eagle of Notre Dame.

Rockne was more than a football coach. He became an American institution. His teams at Notre Dame were not only the greatest in the nation but also the pets of all the people. They played the best teams everywhere, and lost only twelve games in the thirteen years he coached. For five seasons, Notre Dame was unbeaten. Under Rockne, Notre Dame and victory were all but synonymous.

Rockne's way with his players was compounded of magic and wisdom. His locker-room pep talks were replete with dramatics, psychology, scorn, thunder and humor. No coach ever produced so many All-American stars as Rockne, and no coach seemed able to implant in his men so much of his own capacity to lead. Many of his players became coaches themselves, and all the members of two of his undefeated championship teams—the 1921 and 1924 elevens—graduated to the coaching ranks to the last man. As coach and character builder, as leader and teacher, Knute Rockne stood out as the most successful coach in the history of college football.

It was Rockne, the Bald Eagle of Notre Dame, who must be credited with making football big business with enormous stadiums and tremendous crowds that piled into them on autumn Saturday afternoons. The exploits of Notre Dame and Knute Rockne fired the enthusiasm of the nation's football fans, and millions of them turned out during the short intercollegiate season to see the big games. Nowhere were there bigger crowds or higher excitement than where Notre Dame's Fighting Irish came to play.

As the years pass since the untimely death of football's Bald Eagle, the stories and anecdotes about him multiply and spread. Tales of his colorful personality, his influence on the boys who played for him and worshiped him, his revolutionary changes in the game, and his use of daring strategy are heard again and again. But at the heart of his greatness was his fanatical insistence on perfection in play. Rockne believed, and impressed it always on his players, that every play, if perfectly executed, could go for a touchdown. He did not believe that sheer size took the place of skill. As proof, there is the fact that one of the astounding features of the finest backfield he ever developed—the so-called Four Horsemen of the 1924 team—averaged only 158 pounds in weight. For bulk, he substituted speed. For force, he used skill and deception. Always he demanded the most intense practice and drill. To this day, the Notre Dame team is a thing of beauty and perfection, of timing and sharpness of execution. The mark of Knute Rockne's teaching is so impressed on the character of Notre Dame football that it is as though the master were still at the helm.

Knute Rockne has been gone from the football fields of America since 1931. The years have only made more indelible the legend he created. He sleeps now in a cemetery close to the Notre Dame campus he loved so well. He sleeps, but football, the game he did so much to enrich with his magnetic personality, his wisdom and leadership, is all the greater for having known Knute Rockne.

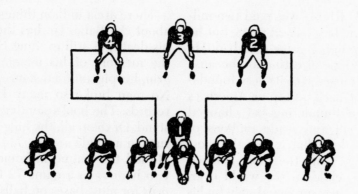

Sultan of Swat

BABE RUTH

GEORGE HERMAN RUTH was paid two million dollars for playing baseball 22 years, but he was the biggest bargain the game ever had. He took a sport on the verge of extinction because of scandals that had rocked it to its very foundations and put it right back on top as America's favorite pastime. His thundering bat changed the nature of baseball and made millions of people who had no idea what it was the most ardent of fans. He became the most beloved figure in the eyes of children the world over, and their love for him was surpassed only by his love for them. He broke a sackful of records over the years, but even if every one of them eventually is beaten and his name is erased from the record books, his will never be less than the biggest name baseball ever had. He was, in short, the one and only, the incomparable Babe Ruth, Sultan of Swat, Lord of Larrupers, King of Clout, the miracle man who lifted baseball out of an early grave and restored it to life.

There are a million things that can be written about the Babe. He has the power, years after his death, of still exciting the imagination with the memory of his mincing walk, his homely grin, his pigeon-toed stance, above all, his feats. No man broke so many long-distance hitting records. The books say that 56 of his marks still stand. Of them all, the biggest are two: 60 home runs in a single season, 714 in his entire career. He led the league in homers 12 times. He hit two homers in a game 72 times. He holds records for most bases on balls, in a season or for a lifetime.

And Babe Ruth did everything big. He ate big, he laughed big, he earned big, he spent big, he hit big—and he struck out big. During his career, they sent him back empty-handed to the dugout with 1,330 strike-outs, also a record. But the fans loved it even when he missed. That mighty swing was something wonderful to behold no matter whether it connected or not.

110

To understand the Babe's fierce devotion to kids, it is necessary to go back to his own childhood. He started life as a child roaming the slum streets of Baltimore, scratching for food wherever he could find it. Life was rough, and the Babe was growing up rough, too. Then one day he was sent to St. Mary's Industrial School, a home for orphans and incorrigibles, where he was set to work to learn the tailor's trade. He learned a little about needle and thread—but he learned a lot more about baseball. Brother Paul, superintendant of the institution, soon saw that he had a boy with marked ability in young George Herman Ruth. He called in his friend, Jack Dunn, owner-manager of the Baltimore Orioles. Dunn hired the boy to play baseball—and paid him $600 a year. But to get him from the orphanage, Dunn had to assume full responsibility for the boy. He did so by adopting him —and thereby created a nickname that has become world-famous.

When Ruth joined the Orioles, he was subjected to the usual hazing and rough handling by the veteran players on the team. One morning, the coach gathered the players together. "Lay off that kid," he warned them. "Don't forget, he's Dunn's babe."

Ruth blossomed out as a pitcher with the minor leaguers and Dunn sold him to the Boston Red Sox for a paltry $2,900. With Boston, the Babe pitched and batted the club to three pennants in five years. He led the American League in winning percentage one year, in earned runs the next. In the 1916 and 1918 World Series he set a record by pitching 29 consecutive shutout innings, a mark that has never been equaled or beaten.

Ruth broke the home-run record with 29 four-masters in 1919. The New York Yankees bought him from Boston and the Babe proceeded to tear up all the clouting records in the books. Home runs flowed from his big bat with thundering regularity. Then, in 1922, Babe came to a low point in his career. Never a stickler for training rules, he began to slip badly. He drew a fine of $5,000, biggest ever assessed against a player. Friends, including Brother Paul, went to work on the Babe. As suddenly as he had begun to slip, Babe began to come back. And his peak was reached in 1927 when he set his fabulous record of 60 home runs for the season.

It was in 1932 that Babe Ruth called the shot that echoed round the world. In the World Series that year, the Chicago Cubs were riding the aging Babe unmercifully. Babe waddled to the plate to the accompaniment of a barrage of boos and catcalls from the enemy bench. He paused in the batter's box, then dramatically pointed his big club toward the distant center-field bleachers. A moment later came the pitch. There was a resounding crack. Away sailed the ball to nestle in the exact spot that Ruth had indicated. The Cub bench fell strangely silent, awed by the great man's answer to their taunts.

There are literally thousands of kids all over the land who are grateful today for the visits Babe paid them in hospitals and sickbeds. Many of them owe their very existence to the big lovable guy who would drop anything he was doing to call on them and help them get well.

In the closing years of his life, Babe was stricken with a deadly illness. He himself was not aware that his days were numbered as he grew weaker and weaker. His big rumbling voice had vanished to a growling whisper when one day his nurse came into his sickroom. She was startled to see the big fellow, now thin and shrunken to half his size, out of his bed and trying to walk across the room.

"Where are you going?" she asked.

The Babe smiled a little. "Not far," whispered Babe Ruth in his familiarly husky voice. "I'm just going over the valley."

Those were his last words. An hour later, he was dead, at 52. The millions who had prayed for his recovery could now do no more than weep for their hero. Baseball's greatest player was no more.

EARL SANDE

A Handy Guy

GREAT JOCKEYS come and go. Each makes his mark, but none has won more hearts than Earl Sande. When he rode he was more than just another boy on a horse—he was a shining symbol of his time. In the roaring twenties, Earl Sande was one of the great figures who gave the era the name of Golden Age of Sports.

In 1916, Earl was an unknown kid working around the stables at a leaky-roof track in Arizona. The youngster did all sorts of menial tasks at the track. He cleaned stalls, curried horses, ran errands—and once in a while he was allowed to exercise a horse.

Then one day Sande was given his chance. The occasion was the annual Arizona Fair. First there was to be a big military review—and then Sande was to ride in his first race!

The military review may have been a magnificent show, but Earl had no mind for anything but the race in which he was going to ride. Six horses were entered in the contest. And Earl Sande was determined to make a strong impression.

When the military review ended, the horses were called to the post. They lined up at the start. In a moment, the signal came. Off went the horses, pounding for the first turn. Sande, crouched low over the neck of his mount, peered ahead, looking for a chance to sneak into the lead.

As they went into the last turn, Sande had his horse in front. It looked like a sure victory for the little novice in his first race. And then it happened.

When the military review ended, a cannon had been left in the infield near the head of the stretch. Thinking there was plenty of time, a squad of soldiers were busy trying to haul the cannon away. As the horses thundered into the home stretch, the soldiers were dragging the big field piece across the track itself.

Someone had miscalculated badly. Hearing the horses bearing down on them, the soldiers fled in panic, leaving the cannon in the middle of the track, in the path of the onrushing horses.

Earl Sande saw the big field piece in front of

him and tried to swerve his horse out of the way. But it was too late to change direction. Sande and horse smashed head-on into the obstacle.

The horse was killed instantly. Sande was flung to the track with sickening impact. The horses running second, third and fourth also slammed into the cannon. Only the last horse, far in the rear, managed to escape injury.

Sande was carried off to the hospital. It was a bitter beginning for the little jockey who was to become so famous. When he recovered after weeks of suffering, Sande resolutely pushed the memory of his first race aside. He was determined to go on with his career.

Over the years, Earl Sande rode more than 5,000 mounts. He won 972 races and became America's most beloved jockey. Among his victories he counted three Kentucky Derbies and five Belmont Stakes.

One day in 1924, Earl was riding at glamorous Saratoga. There was a pile-up at one of the turns during a race, and Sande was pulled out of the wreckage more dead than alive. Several ribs were broken, his collarbone was snapped, his left leg was crushed. Doctors prepared to amputate the leg.

"Please don't," begged Earl. "If I can't ride again, I'd rather die."

Somehow, Sande survived his terrible injuries. A few months later, he was riding again. And the following spring, Sande won his greatest race—the Kentucky Derby of 1925, on Flying Ebony.

By the time Earl Sande decided to call it a day, his name was known everywhere. No jockey had made such an impression on public and press. The wonderful runt with the heart of steel had even been immortalized in a poem —Damon Runyon's famous sport classic, "A Handy Guy Like Sande."

Again and again, little Earl Sande, one of the greatest saddlesmiths in racing history, amazed the sports world with his courageous comebacks. Even when his wife died after only a few years of wedded bliss, and even when he lost his life's savings in the market crash—more than a quarter-of-a-million dollars—Sande came back. He took the buffeting of fate in stride.

In 1954, Earl Sande staged his most amazing comeback. After twenty-one years out of the saddle, like a ghost out of the past, Earl Sande reappeared on a race track, decked out in the garish work-clothes of the jockey—to ride again. The day he came back as a jockey, he was all of 54.

WILBUR SHAW
Speedway Daredevil

AS A BOY, Wilbur Shaw grew up with the thunder of motors in his ears. Living within walking distance of the world-famous Indianapolis Speedway, the youngster spent every moment he could spare within earshot of the racing cars, listening to the grease-covered mechanics and daredevils of the road talking shop. And he vowed to himself that some day he too would race on the Speedway and win the highest honor that can come to an automobile racing driver.

When he was 18, Shaw built a racing car from second-hand parts given him by a friendly garage owner. He entered the little car in his first dirt-track race. A few minutes after the start, Wilbur Shaw was sitting by the side of the road in a broken-down piece of junk. The little car had collapsed after a lap or two.

But by 1927, half-a-dozen years later, Shaw made his debut in the grueling 500-mile Indianapolis race, most famous in the world. To everyone's astonishment, including his own, he roared to a fourth-place finish. After that first attempt, nothing could keep him from the racing cars. Fourteen times he raced in the famed annual classic. Once in a while he brushed sleeves with death as the car he drove crashed

or burst into flames. Then, in 1936, he designed a strange-looking car he called the "Vacuum Cleaner." It brought him only seventh place at Indianapolis. But in 1937 he finally reached the goal he had so long been seeking. He won the big 500-mile Memorial Day race. A life's ambition was realized.

But it was not enough. Two years later, Shaw performed the feat of winning the big race a second time. And it might have been his third success in a row had not a peculiar thing happened in the grind of 1938. In that race, he was winging along comfortably in the lead when he stopped for a moment to check up with his pit crew. A spectator grabbed Shaw just as he was about to get back into his car to resume the race. The spectator wanted only to praise the great driver for his efforts, and Shaw had a great deal of trouble disentangling himself. At last his pit crew interceded and pushed the spectator away. But Shaw had lost a precious 25 seconds by the delay. And it was by a mere 18 seconds that he missed winning the race!

After winning the 1939 race, Shaw was the most famous and wealthiest of all the Speedway drivers. Now 37, he was a veteran of the track with no worlds left to conquer. But Shaw wanted to show that he was still the best. And prove it he did, by going out before 152,000 howling fans to win the big grind for the third time and the second year in a row, a feat never before accomplished by any racing car driver.

Full of honors as America's, perhaps the world's, greatest racing car driver, Wilbur Shaw later became the president of the Indianapolis Speedway. Over the years, it fell to him to watch the furiously speeding drivers on the track below him on other Memorial Days. But never could they have thrilled him as much as when he himself showed the way in the toughest, most grueling automobile race in the world.

EDDIE SHORE
Firebrand of the Ice

A PLAYER who had been felled in the heat of action by Eddie Shore, hockey's roughest, toughest and most colorful star of his day, had only this to say to the man who had almost killed him on the ice: "Eddie, you're the most brutal player that ever lived—but the cleanest. Don't feel bad about me. It's all in the game." Fortunately, the man recovered. But he never played again.

No one knew better than Eddie Shore what it cost a man to play ice hockey. Born on a ranch in Canada, he began to play the game at college. Later he joined the Regina hockey team in Calgary. As a newcomer, Shore was a marked man in his first game against one of Regina's most powerful opponents. As soon as he took the ice, the youngster knew he was in for it. Rival players swooped down on him in solid phalanxes, hitting the rookie with everything they had—knees, elbows, shoulders, sticks and skates.

But nothing they did to him could make Eddie Shore quit. His own teammates marveled to see him continue in the game in spite of the battering he was taking. When the match was over, they checked over the damage that had been done to their new player. The list of injuries was a formidable one. He had a broken nose, several broken teeth, a cracked collar bone and a brain concussion. But he had proved himself. Eddie Shore was a hockey player.

After that initial experience, Shore went on to become not only the greatest but also the most feared player in ice hockey. Nothing ever stopped him, nothing scared him. While starring with Boston for many years, he also became the highest paid player in the game. Season after season saw him chosen for the All-Star team and he was one of the first to be named to Hockey's Hall of Fame.

The dangerous and violent Eddie Shore played hockey like a man possessed. Entirely oblivious to pain and injury, he collected over the years the most extensive damage ever handed out to a hockey player. His body was a mass of scars that criss-crossed their way from head to foot. He suffered, at one time or another, a serious spinal injury, many broken bones, a gashed head, a fractured jaw. And, by the time he quit, all the teeth had been knocked out of his head. His scalp carried 19 scars as evidence that he had been to the hockey wars. All in all, Eddie Shore had had enough gashes and cuts to require the fantastic total of 600 stitches to close them up.

Eddie Shore hurt many an opponent because he could not play the game gently—but the firebrand of hockey did not escape the fires he set without being himself badly scorched!

WILLIE SHOEMAKER
Silent Shoe

BY THE TIME he reached his tenth birthday, Willie Shoemaker was faced by a sad but inevitable fact. Although he was the eldest of five boys in his family, he would always be the smallest of the lot. For poor Willie had never grown like the others. Always tiny and thin, he weighed barely 90 pounds when he was entering high school in California. There, despite his small size and low weight, he managed to star in boxing and wrestling, never once being defeated in high school competition. But he didn't grow. No matter what he did, he stayed small.

After school hours, Willie worked on a ranch where he helped break yearlings. But he was only marking time until he grew up and could decide what to do with his life. When he admitted at last that 4 feet, 11 inches and 90 pounds was as far as he was ever going to go physically, he made a bold decision. He left school and went to work as an exercise boy at the Bay Meadows race track. He was only 16, but he had made up his mind that he was going to become a jockey.

In his very first year, Willie established himself solidly in his new career. He rode 219 winners and earned some $40,000 for himself. Some thought the new boy was only a flash in the pan. But he said nothing in defense of his newly found fame. He kept to himself and acted as if nothing unusual had happened in his life. "Silent Shoe" they nicknamed this cold, emotionless boy—59 inches tall.

It was in 1950 when Willie Shoemaker really captured the headlines as one of America's great jockeys. That year, he staged a stirring duel with Joe Culmone for the American riding championship. He established a record for winning mounts in a season at 388, though he had to share his glory and that record with his rival.

Meanwhile, his earnings had doubled over those of his first year in the saddle.

By this time there was no question in anyone's mind that Silent Shoe was truly one of the greats of the turf. The following year, this boy who tried to avoid the limelight won $1,329,890 in purses for the fortunate owners of his mounts while winning 257 races. In 1952 he again passed the million-dollar mark while winning 315 races. But now there were few startling headlines for the little fellow from California. He threatened no records and performed nothing especially sensational. At 21, Willie Shoemaker had become just another good jockey. But in 1953, he really blossomed out to stand alone in turf glory. He booted home the incredible total of 450 winners for the year to become the first and only jockey in history to ride to victory more than 400 times in a single season of horse racing. And while creating this astounding record which may never be topped, he also earned $120,000 for his year's work at riding winning race horses.

At 22, after only five years of riding race horses, Willie Shoemaker stood at an envious peak in his life—hailed by the turf world as the perfect jockey, and with no records to break but his own!

116

TOD SLOAN

A Yankee Doodle Dandy

TOD SLOAN was a tiny, skinny, pinch-faced mite of a man when he left Kokomo, Indiana, to seek fame and fortune as a jockey. The beady-eyed little fellow was a sensation from the start. Having abnormally short legs, Sloan rode his horse high up on the neck and used short stirrups, a style that soon became the accepted one for most American and English riders. But it was his daring and almost reckless courage that made him so outstanding a jockey. He could pilot a galloping horse through the eye of a needle. And no finer judge of pace could be found anywhere on a race track. He could control the wildest horse with a mere touch of his hands and the most stubborn and unwilling of animals would run for him when they would run for no one else.

Tod Sloan became the most famous jockey in America, winning race after race in sensational fashion. Soon he became the idol of the turf world. And wherever there was joy and gaiety there was the Kokomo Kid, a long black stogie between his teeth, laughing, living and spending with rash abandon.

Sloan bought himself a yacht and built himself a palatial home out of his enormous earnings on the turf. Night after night, he threw

thousand-dollar parties, and famous men and women from every walk of life flocked to them. He numbered his friends by the thousands and his admirers were legion.

But he soon tired of the fame and adulation he had won in his homeland. The Kokomo Kid suddenly picked up and left for England. There, too, he became in a short while the darling of the public. And he lived like royalty. His wardrobe of 25 trunks filled a hotel suite and contained the best clothes tailored for him by the smartest tailors in London. His hotel quarters cost him $300 a day. Not only did he number dukes, earls and viscounts among his closest friends, but also the whole world of art, music and literature.

At the peak of his fame as a jockey, Tod Sloan commanded fantastic fees to ride. The millionaire racing man, William C. Whitney, paid him $30,000 to ride his favorite colt in a big race. And when the Kokomo Kid won for Mr. Whitney, there was another $10,000 for him to sweeten the pot.

And Tod ruled the turf with a will of iron. When a famous actress, a friend of Tod's, was late one day to see him ride in an important stake, Sloan held up the race for an hour until he could see her come into the clubhouse. Then he went out and won the race!

Tod Sloan was the first rider to earn over a million dollars. However, money and fame mixed to make a clown of the incomparable jockey. At the very height of his career, Sloan was obliged to leave England when his antics became more than the turf fans could tolerate. He drifted on to France, Belgium and other parts of Europe. He continued to ride with some success, but it was becoming clear to all that his star was fading fast. The day finally came when Tod Sloan sailed for America. But his return was not a triumphal one. Tod Sloan was only a washed-up jockey.

He took to drifting from track to track in his search for horses to ride. They were fewer and farther between. Slowly his fortune evaporated, as did all the friends who had once gathered under fair skies to do him homage. Before long, the first millionaire jockey in turf history was living in a shabby hotel room, alone and deserted, subsisting on handouts.

Tod Sloan was still hoping for the break that would catapult him back to the top as the pre-mier jockey of the age when he rode his last ride on December 21, 1933. But his hands were not on the reins, his feet not in the stirrups. The mighty mite's last ride was in a gray hearse to his grave. The only ones to mourn him on his way were a broken-down prizefighter, a faded baseball player, a forgotten old actor and a sentimental sports writer. And if there were no others to mourn the passing of history's most colorful jockey, at least the skies wept with rain as he was lowered into his last resting place.

Even though the turf world, ever in search of new heroes, saw fit to forget the Kokomo Kid, most fabulous of jockeys, the rollicking spirit of this little man of the saddle remains. The famous song and dance man of the American stage, George M. Cohan, saw to that when he wrote a musical comedy based on the life and times of the cocky little rider. From that stage play came a treasured song which America still sings. The fame of Tod Sloan, the jockey, is immortalized in the song, "I'm a Yankee Doodle Dandy."

TRIS SPEAKER
The Gray Eagle

THERE NEVER WAS a better centerfielder in all baseball than Tris Speaker. The "Gray Eagle," as he came to be known, did more than anyone else in the game to revolutionize outfield play. Playing the shortest center field possible, only a few steps behind second base, he could when necessary go back farther and faster than any man who ever lived. Because he did play so close, he was unique as the only outfielder to make two unassisted double plays in a season, and the only one to make that unusual twin-killing in a World Series, doing so in 1912 against the New York Giants.

For 22 years Tris Speaker starred in the major leagues as one of the greatest fielders, hitters and base-runners. His name and deeds still dot the record books and he is, of course, one of that handful of immortals who dwell in baseball's Hall of Fame at historic Cooperstown.

The Gray Eagle of baseball was born Tristram E. Speaker in Hubbard City, Texas, the only boy in a family of seven. Tris was a wild youngster with a gift for getting himself into trouble. He made his start in baseball as a left-handed pitcher with Cleburne of the North Texas League. He pitched 7 times and lost 7 times. One afternoon, after he had lost dis-

astrously by a score of 24–6, his manager told him to pack up and get out, that he would never amount to anything in baseball. Tris Speaker sadly agreed to give up—pitching, that is.

He did not give up baseball. He became an outfielder. A Pittsburgh scout who watched him one day was sufficiently impressed by the young unknown to want to sign him up. But Pittsburgh's owner refused to hire Speaker after learning that he smoked. He did not feel that rookies should smoke.

A little later, the Boston Red Sox bought Tris Speaker for a measly $800. When he batted only .158 for seven games, Speaker was turned over to Little Rock for the season in payment of Boston's use of the local ballpark during spring training. But the next year Tris was back up with the Red Sox to stay. Over the years, with Boston and Cleveland, he made a number of extraordinary records. His 22-year batting average was .344. He made a total of 3,515 hits, including a record 793 doubles, 433 stolen bases and 1,146 bases on balls. As a fielder, he established notable marks of 35 assists in both 1909 and 1912. During his major league career he struck out only 222 times. And he was past 37 when he made the astonishing record of batting .389 for a full season of play at Cleveland.

Not only did Tris Speaker win immortal renown as the player who became known as Cleveland's "fifth infielder." He was good enough as a manager to bring the Indians a league pennant in 1920 and then win the world championship in a thrilling World Series against Brooklyn.

The Dean of Football Coaches

AMOS ALONZO STAGG

IT WAS A WARM summer's day back in 1892. Two men met in New York at a famous hotel for lunch. One of them was the nationally known Dr. Harper, recently appointed president of the new University of Chicago. The other was a handsome young athlete named Amos Alonzo Stagg, famous at Yale as a pitcher on the baseball team, more noted as an end on the football team. Stagg had been elected to the first All-American team in 1889 by Walter Camp. He had been out of Yale for two years and had since been coaching and teaching at Springfield College.

Dr. Harper liked the looks of this young man. As lunch ended, he made his proposition. "I'd like you to join us at the University of Chicago," he said. "We're just beginning to organize a faculty and you seem like the sort we'd like to build with." He hesitated. "I can pay you $1,500 a year."

Stagg remained silent.

"Make it $2,500 and an associate professorship in physical education," said Dr. Harper. "Will you come, Stagg?"

Stagg looked up. "Dr. Harper," he began slowly, "you know I studied for the ministry."

Dr. Harper nodded.

"I think I can do as much good in athletics as in the pulpit," went on Stagg. "I'll be happy to come to Chicago if you let me combine athletics and physical education in one department."

The two men shook hands on it. Stagg returned to Springfield to get his things together. And soon he was on his way to Chicago to be-

come a teacher and coach at a brand-new university at a time when the now-famous Chicago Midway was only a cow pasture. The former shoemaker's son who had made such a remarkable record as an athlete at Yale little knew what was in store for him.

At the University of Chicago, Amos Alonzo Stagg took over the coaching of baseball and track. But most important of all, he took over the football squad.

Stagg stayed at Chicago for the stretch of 41 years. He became nothing less than a Chicago landmark. Some of the football teams he developed were among the greatest in the land. Along the way, Stagg turned out scores of great players. And he added so much to the strategy and technique of the game that he practically revolutionized football.

After 41 seasons, Amos Alonzo Stagg reached his 71st birthday. The decades that had passed so quickly had been good ones for Stagg as well as the University of Chicago. As a coach, his position was close to the very top. As a university, Chicago stood in a similar position.

Nevertheless, Stagg was 71, and the university felt it was time for him to retire from the game. Stagg accepted the decision gracefully. But he did not retire. "I never knew more about football than I know now," he said. "I'm too young to quit." And he looked around for more worlds to conquer.

An offer came to coach the football team of the little College of the Pacific in Stockton, California. Stagg promptly packed his bags, bade Chicago a fond farewell and went off to start a new career as a football coach.

For 13 years, Amos Alonzo Stagg molded fine teams at the little West Coast college. And while there, at the ripe age of 81, he was voted college football coach of the year by the nation's football coaches and writers.

At the close of the 1946 season, Stagg left the College of the Pacific. It was believed on all sides that the old man had finally decided to retire from the ranks of football coaches. But

Stagg was not thinking of quitting even then. If he knew too much to retire at 71, how much more did he know about football at 84?

The only problem was where to go. Stagg came east again to coach at Susquehanna University, even smaller than the College of the Pacific. He made only one concession to encroaching age. He shared the chores of coaching with another man—his own son.

Stagg stayed on at Susquehanna for years, still carrying on the work he had been doing all his life. When he was 90 years old, he had long since earned the honor of being known as the dean of all football coaches—and he was still coaching a football team. It was his 63rd consecutive year at the reins—the longest span of gridiron leadership in the game's annals.

CASEY STENGEL

Casey at the Helm

FOR YEARS, Casey Stengel laughed his way through baseball, and the world had laughed along with him. As a player, he had been famous for his antics, his wit, his gags, and his anecdotes. As a manager, he had been noted particularly for piloting the worst teams any club had ever fielded. As a club president, Casey had fired himself as manager so he could take a better job elsewhere. As a dentist when a young man, his left-handedness had proved too great a handicap to overcome.

A man like that should have been allowed mercifully to live out his life in peace as a chronic failure and misfit who had been given a lot of chances but had not been able to capitalize on any of them. Instead, Casey finally struck the richest lode of gold in the baseball world. He became the manager of the New York Yankees in the spring of 1949. He won a pennant that year and the World Series that followed. And in '50, '51, '52 and '53, Casey Stengel repeated that performance, winning in the five years exactly five pennants and five World Series, a feat that has never in history been equaled by any manager.

Some three decades have passed since Charles D. Stengel came up to the big time as a hard-hitting outfielder with the Brooklyn Dodgers and picked up his nickname that stuck. From the very beginning, Casey was a zany—and the yarns that have come down from those dim beginnings are legion—and hilarious. There was the time Casey was in a tight and important game at Ebbets Field, and a vast crowd was on hand to see the Dodgers win. Since Casey was playing with the visiting Pittsburgh Pirates instead of his former club, the crowd roundly booed their former hero as he came to bat for the first time. Casey turned to the plate umpire and asked for time. Then he bowed to the howling mob, lifted his cap, and revealed to the startled onlookers a sparrow poised on top of his head. There was a flutter and the sparrow flew away. The boos turned to laughs.

There were hundreds more such madcap incidents in which the fun-loving Stengel was a ringleader. Overshadowed by his pranks were some fine playing accomplishments by the big-eared, blue-eyed Stengel. For example, twice in World Series he won games for the New York

122

Giants with home runs. He played 14 years in the majors, for Brooklyn, New York, Pittsburgh and Philadelphia.

As noted, his managing career was a dud for many years. He shuttled back and forth between minor and major league clubs. When he had a good squad he did well. When he had a poor one, as he did so often, there were only the laughs to compensate for the misery of finishing in the second division.

But everybody knew Casey Stengel had something. And that faith in the ability of Casey Stengel to run a ball club successfully was more than justified when the New York Yankees astounded the baseball world by calling on him to manage in 1949. With five successive pennants and five successive World Series in his belt, there can never again be a question as to whether Casey Stengel is a clown or one of baseball's greatest managers. There won't be a better one until his consecutive victory record is broken—and the only one likely to do that is old Casey Stengel himself!

The
Boston Strong Boy

JOHN L. SULLIVAN

SEPTEMBER 7, 1892 was a black day for Boston, even blacker, perhaps, than the day of the infamous Massacre of 1770. For in 1892, the great and beloved John L. Sullivan, native of Roxbury, a Boston suburb, crashed in defeat at the hands of a younger and more nimble adversary in a bout for the heavyweight championship of the world. For ten years, the great John L. had held sway over the fistic world. They were ten years of greatness, ten years of triumph over all opponents, ten years of glory for the citizens of Boston whose greatest hero John L. Sullivan had been.

It was on February 7, 1882 that John L. Sullivan had wrenched the bare-knuckle championship from one Paddy Ryan and begun his decade of fistic invulnerability. The new champion was to be the last of the bare-knuckle kings, and to carry that title to his grave, for no one ever beat him under bare-knuckle rules after he won the crown.

It was a time when America was stirring with new-found greatness, and Sullivan made a fitting champion for the period. For there was something about the swashbuckling champ that warmed the hearts of the people of America. His swaggering style, the spectacular nature of his victories, his enormous gusto and love for

life endeared him to everybody. And when, as champion, John L. boasted wherever he went, "I can lick any man in the world!" the boast was no bigger than the land he lived in. Sullivan and America were prepared to take on anybody, each in its own way.

John L. Sullivan was the nation's first universal sports hero. He had become a fighter almost by accident when he accepted a challenge to come up and try to last three rounds with a thick-set pugilist on a theater stage. John L., who stood 5 feet, 10½ inches, and weighed about 195 pounds, was a 19-year-old youth when he stepped up on the stage. He knocked out the pug in one short round. It was the beginning of a spectacular career which would see him become the last of the bare-knuckle title-holders and the first recognized champion with boxing gloves. Previously, he had almost become a professional baseball player. The fabulous Cincinnati Red Stockings had offered John L., who had played some semi-pro ball, $1,500 to come pitch for them. Only 16 at the time, John L. saw fit to turn the offer down. After all, he could earn as much as $100 a week even in those days by playing for the semi-pros.

After John L. became a prizefighter, his trade led him to many odd places. One day he might fight on a barge, another in the backroom of a saloon, on a stage, or in a clearing in the woods. It made no difference to him. He swaggered along, tossing pennies to the kids who lined his way, roaring greetings to his friends and curses at his enemies. John L. lived his life to the full.

As champion, John L. made a grand tour of Europe. In England he was a sensation, receiving ovation after ovation from the usually restrained British. No other American was ever to be so warmly received. The Prince of Wales became his bosom pal. And in France too, John L. was greeted like a king. All the world loved him.

Back in America, John L. took to touring the land to show the people what a great fighter he was. In one year, he gave as many as 200 exhibitions of his prowess, meeting anyone who dared to fight him. To any man who could last four rounds, he offered a standing prize of $500. Many were tempted to climb into the ring with the formidable champion. Not once did Sullivan have to pay out money to a challenger. There was one series of exhibitions in which John L. knocked out 60 bold aspirants for the $500 in a row, all in the very first round!

Then came the black day, the day all Boston mourned and the bells tolled sadly the end of a great champion's reign. A man named James J. Corbett had danced and feinted his way to victory over Sullivan. The mighty champion, worn down to a helpless hulk by the elusive Corbett, had been brought to his knees in the 21st round.

Four men carried John L. back to his corner. In the arena, every eye wept at the fall of the beloved idol. When Sullivan revived, he walked unassisted to the ropes and raised his arm for silence. "My friends," he said, and his roar was almost a whisper, "I have fought once too often. But if I had to get licked, I'm glad it was by an American! Yours truly, John L. Sullivan."

John L. had earned barely more than $100,-000 as a fighter, but his lecture tours, his acting and exhibitions, had brought him well over a million dollars. In his last years, he toured the country lecturing on the good life and the evils of the world. However, the great ex-champion died without a penny to his name. Only his old sparring partner was at his bedside when the end came. It took ten strong men to carry the great casket that held his last remains. The great John L. was borne to his last resting place in the Roxbury cemetery. There he lies to this day, secure in the hearts of the American people as their first heavyweight champion of the world.

JIM THORPE

The Fabulous Indian

THE SCENE was Stockholm, Sweden. The year was 1912. In the dressing rooms of the Olympic stadium, some athletes were changing from track clothes to street attire. They had just come in from the field where they had competed in the most gruelling of all Olympic events, the decathlon.

The door to the dressing room opened suddenly and a tall man entered. He looked around him until his glance fell on a copper-skinned, powerfully-built athlete. Then he strode across the room and stuck out his hand.

"Sir," he said, "you are the greatest athlete in the world. I would consider it an honor to shake your hand."

The big athlete smiled and rose to his feet. The two shook hands and then the tall visitor left the room.

That scene has become a legend in sports. The King of Sweden had come in to pay tribute to Jim Thorpe.

The King of Sweden was entirely justified in seeking out and congratulating Jim Thorpe. The American Indian was unquestionably the greatest all-around athlete the world has yet seen. There was no sport, no game, he could not play superlatively well. Jim Thorpe could do everything.

By winning the pentathlon and decathlon at the 1912 Olympics, (five events in one and ten in the other) big Jim Thorpe was only bringing to a climax all the great things he had ever done in track and field. Ever since the day he had first appeared, an 18-year-old Sac and Fox Indian boy from an Oklahoma reservation, he had been a one-man track team. On one occasion, Jim Thorpe and four schoolmates at the Carlisle Indian School turned up to meet Lafayette College in a track meet. The Lafayette coach was furious. "What do you mean, you're the Carlisle track team? Do you five fellows expect to compete against my 47-man squad?"

"I usually come with only two others," replied Thorpe imperturbably. "We'll manage all right."

All Jim did that day was win the 100-yard dash, the pole vault, the high jump, the shot-put, the running broad jump and the 220-yard dash. Needless to say, Jim Thorpe, the one-man track team, defeated Lafayette by a lop-sided score.

Jim Thorpe was football's greatest player. At Carlisle, he was the kingpin of one of the most powerful football aggregations of all time. Against Harvard one afternoon, in the days when the Crimson ruled the world of football, Thorpe, his legs swathed in bandages because of the pounding he had taken in earlier games, not only scored a touchdown but also kicked four field goals from beyond the 40-yard line. He scored all the points for winning Carlisle that day.

Against a mighty Army team, big Jim received the opening kick-off and sped 95 yards for a touchdown. Carlisle was adjudged offside and the run was nullified. Again the West Pointers kicked off. This time Jim took the ball on his own goal line and ran 100 yards for the touchdown!

Thorpe was almost the whole Carlisle team. In a game, he was impervious to injury. Everytime his shoe crashed against the ball, it traveled from 60 to 70 yards. There were times when he kicked more than 80 yards on the fly. He was the greatest all-around backfield player ever seen on a football field. Long touchdown runs flowed from Jim Thorpe's legs in an endless stream of spectacular plays. He scored two or three touchdowns in every game he played.

As a professional, Jim Thorpe played football for 20 years. So powerful a runner was he, so formidable a line-smasher, that no one ever dared to take up his standing offer to pay $1000 to any team that could keep him from gaining ten yards in four downs.

His pro football exploits would have been career enough for any other man, but Thorpe was a top-flight baseball player too. He starred as an outfielder with the New York Giants, the Boston Braves, and the Cincinnati Reds. In eight years of big-league play he compiled a hefty lifetime batting average of .320.

Baseball, football and track were not the only sports in which the big Indian excelled. He was a great star in at least a dozen other fields of athletics. But all his glorious achievements turned to ashes for the marvelous all-around

champion of sports. After the Olympic games in which he performed so brilliantly, it was learned that he had played for a brief time semi-pro ball for $25 a week, while a student at Carlisle. His medals were taken from him and his Olympic records were removed from the books. They were never restored to him, despite worldwide agitation.

During his last years, Jim was all but forgotten. Living in deepest poverty, sick and neglected, he even at one time had to dig ditches to keep body and soul together. And, when he was only 64, Jim Thorpe was found dead on the floor of his one-room trailer. His great heart had given out. Forty-six years had passed since the big Indian had first appeared on the Carlisle Indian School campus to begin his fantastic career. The end was bitter, but the legend of big Jim Thorpe, greatest in football, track's one-man team, glorious Olympic champion, major league ballplayer, will live forever in the memories of all the followers of sports.

No wonder the sport historians unanimously voted him the greatest football player and the greatest all-around athlete of the 20th century!

BILL TILDEN

Giant of the Court

IN AN ERA that was rightfully called the Golden Age of Sports, "Big Bill" Tilden towered above other tennis players like a giant in an age of pygmies.

William Tatum Tilden II came of blueblood stock, a Philadelphian who had been raised by a pair of maiden aunts because he had lost his parents at an early age. As a tennis player in his youth, he looked like a hopeless failure. But he played so unceasingly, and with such frenzy, that he earned the name of "nut." Everyone thought he was crazy for believing there was any future for him on the courts.

At the beginning of his career, Tilden entered many tournaments and rarely, if ever, got past the first round. But he persisted in his wild hope of getting somewhere in tennis. And then, almost suddenly it seemed, the tide changed.

Bill Tilden was 27 when he seemed to blossom out almost overnight as a great tennis player. And, by the time he had finished playing competitive tennis, he proved himself to be the greatest of them all, a master of every shot —a fierce and indomitable fighter, and a showman beyond compare.

In 1923, at the height of his fabulous career, Tilden ran into a fence during a match and bruised a finger on his playing hand. It became infected, and to save his arm, the finger was amputated. The sports world was shocked by the tragedy that had befallen the great player. His amazing tennis career now seemed to be over. But Tilden was an incomparable champion. He emerged from that ordeal, a stronger and more determined tennis champion. Handicapped by the loss of a finger on his playing hand, Tilden developed new grips and new strokes so quickly he soared to the top again as the world's greatest tennis player.

It is hard to describe the effect that Tilden had on an audience when he came strolling nonchalantly out on a court. As soon as he appeared, his tall frame slightly bowed, two or three rackets cradled in his arms, his eyes looking around him with haughty arrogance and supreme confidence, a feeling as if a current of electricity had been released coursed through the stands. No athlete in any field ever had more of this quality of being able to generate excitement in an audience merely by making an appearance. And to this exciting personality, Bill Tilden added such skill at his game, such power and cleverness and speed, that he never let the fans down from their initial excitement.

The cold figures of Tilden's accomplishments go only a little way towards telling the complete story. Beginning when he was 27, Tilden won the United States National crown seven times. For a period of ten years, he was the number one player in the entire world. Wherever there was a tennis title to be won, there was the long-striding Tilden, to win it. Over the years, he covered 750,000 miles to play—the equivalent of girdling the earth 30 times. He won 70 American and international tennis titles. Big Bill had fanatical followings not only in America, but also in France, Italy, Austria, Germany, Belgium, Switzerland, Britain, Australia, New Zealand, and the Middle East. Everywhere he met the best and beat the best on the best days they ever had!

As for the Davis Cup, symbol of world supremacy in tennis, Tilden fought for it and defended it against all comers with the ferocity of a tiger protecting its young. Over a stretch of seven years, he won a phenomenal 13 challenge matches in a row. All told, he won 17 Davis Cup matches between 1920 and 1930, as well as sharing doubles victories four times.

His importance in the game is illustrated by a famous incident. On one occasion, he refused to go to England to play in the famed Wimbledon tournament. The disappointment of his many fans across the water was very great. A clamor went up for Tilden to go, but still he declined. Then, at last, someone was found who could persuade the great star to sail. It took nothing less than a request from the President of the United States, Warren G. Harding, to convince Bill Tilden to accept the Wimbledon invitation. He went to England, played at Wimbledon and won the crown.

When Tilden became a professional in 1931, he blazed a new path of glory through the ranks of play-for-pay. Although he played until he was well into his fifties, he was still one of the world's great tennis players. He earned more than a million dollars but with a careless hand, he tossed it all away.

For thirty years, Bill Tilden played and acted on the tennis courts of the world, and always, he gave a magnificent performance as a champion. He was the friend of kings and statesmen, motion picture stars and most of the celebrities of the world. A slashing and indomitable figure on a tennis court, the astonishing Tilden also made his mark in other fields—as an actor, an author, a playwright and a teacher.

But his private life drew him into scandal and he came to the end of the road with nothing to show for his fabulous career as the idol of millions. At sixty, he was found in a shabby little hotel room—lifeless. Alone and without a friend by his side, his great heart finally had given out. It was a lonely, cruel finish for the incredible William Tatum Tilden, giant of the Golden Age!

TORGER TOKLE
Hero on Skis

WHEN TORGER TOKLE finished high school in his native Norway, he came to the United States. He was 19 years old, entirely unknown in his new home and unable to speak a word of English. But he had a talent in sports that needed no language to be appreciated. Torger Tokle was a ski jumper.

It didn't take Tokle long to make his name known in his adopted land. Soon after his arrival, he established himself as America's greatest ski jumper. To a sport in which Americans showed little interest before his coming, Tokle brought such thrills that it soon attracted spectators by the thousands. For Tokle presented a dramatic spectacle at every ski jumping meet he entered. He demonstrated his specialty in all parts of the country where there was snow and an incline, and his nerve and daring on the slopes were unforgettably breathtaking.

Jumping on Eastern slopes, Tokle soon raised his mark to 133 feet, then 160 and 180 feet. But the Eastern hills were too easy for the Norwegian jumper. In 1941, he paid a visit to Leavenworth, Washington, where the slopes were considerably sharper. There he hung up a new American mark for the death-defying descent by leaping 273 feet. And, in the following year, he went to America's most famous ski jump at Iron Mountain, Michigan, and soared through space for a distance of 289 feet. In addition to setting this record, Tokle shattered 24 different hill records in various parts of the country, and won 42 meets. Never was he outjumped.

Proud as he was of his new-found fame, Torger Tokle was prouder still to call himself an American. In the same year he broke the record, he became an American citizen. As he took the oath, he said in solemn gratitude, "I will make my adopted country proud of me."

Late in 1942, Torger Tokle answered his new homeland's call to arms. He soon became Sgt. Torger Tokle, platoon leader of a skiing company in the 86th Infantry Regiment.

One day in March, 1945, Sergeant Tokle led his men in the scaling of a tremendous ridge in the rugged Italian Apennines to launch a surprise attack on a German garrison. Tokle and his men climbed a snowy mountain some five miles long and 3,500 feet high in one of the most brilliant mountain-climbing operations in military history.

Torger Tokle failed to come through that ordeal. A shell cut him down during the attack and killed him instantly. He died under circumstances which he might well have chosen deliberately, had he had the choice: high on a snowy height, and on skis. The oath he had taken had been kept. His new country could not but be proud of its fledgling citizen who so bravely gave his life to preserve her freedom.

GENE TUNNEY
The Fighting Marine

IT WAS from colorful Greenwich Village in New York City that a husky colorless young clerk with a liking for books went off to war in 1917 with a contingent of Marines. In the service, the young man—Gene Tunney—won himself a little fame by winning the inter-allied boxing tournament in the light heavyweight class. His success in the ring turned Tunney's thoughts to the idea of boxing as a career. When he returned to America after the war, he became a professional boxer.

For three years, Tunney fought with small success in minor or preliminary bouts. The former Marine received little attention from boxing fans generally. When the great Jack Dempsey met the glamorous Frenchman, Georges Carpentier, in July 1921, Tunney appeared obscurely in one of the preliminary bouts. As usual, no one noticed him. All eyes and attention were on the champion who won a brilliant victory.

But a year later, the unknown Marine burst into print with a rash and fantastic challenge. Tunney declared publicly that he wanted to fight the great Dempsey, heavyweight champion of the world. What was more, he was certain that he could lick the Manassa Mauler.

Tunney's challenge was the biggest laugh-getter of the year. A cautious and non-aggressive fighter, he had won the light heavyweight title without causing a ripple in fistic circles. He was known as a handsome young ex-Marine, a man of faultless living habits who liked books, society people and cultural pursuits.

When Gene Tunney finally fought for the world's heavyweight crown, he created the most amazing upset in boxing history. The clever and scientific ex-Marine outboxed the great Dempsey all the way to take a ten-round decision and the title from the champion. For that fight, Tunney earned as much as he had in all his career to that date.

The following year, champion Gene Tunney gave the ex-king of the heavies a return match. For this second meeting, Gene received the highest pay a professional athlete had received for a single performance—the sum of $990,445 for thirty minutes of fighting! The bout was otherwise memorable as the one which Tunney won after taking the famous "long count" as he sat out a knockdown from the fists of the former champion.

Tunney fought only once after beating Dempsey for the second time. He knocked out Tom Heeney in 12 rounds. For this bout, Gene collected a mere half-million dollars. Then he announced his retirement. He left the ring unmarked and a millionaire. But the most striking fact of all was that this colorless fighter was the only heavyweight champion in history to retire permanently from the ring undefeated.

RUBE WADDELL
Baseball's Greatest Clown

THERE WAS ONCE a theory that if a pitcher was left-handed he had to be eccentric, if not downright mad. The man who did most to make the theory look good was George E. Waddell, southpaw hurler in the major leagues near the turn of the century. On the other hand, while he was just as loony and odd as legend insists, he was also the greatest left-handed pitcher in the game.

To the oldtimers who saw Rube Waddell in action on the hill, there never was any question about his greatness. When he attended strictly to business, he was a matchless moundsman. He hurled in the major leagues for 14 years, pitching for five different clubs. Despite his clowning and fantastic capers, Rube was good enough to win 193 games and strike out 2,306 batters. In one season alone, that of 1904, he struck out 349 men in 1,384 innings, a record that stayed in the books for 42 years.

As for his antics, it can only be said that Rube Waddell was a boy who never grew up. He was as likely to disappear from the ball park as he was to stay. He chased fire engines on their way to fires, he joined parades that passed the ball park, he turned handsprings for the kids on the corner. Once, while pitching for Chicago during a hot pennant drive, he vanished altogether. After a frantic search, the whacky southpaw was found peacefully fishing at a secluded country spot. In his spare time, when the fish were not biting to his satisfaction, he was pitching for a local semi-pro baseball team!

So varied and unpredictable were the antics of the Rube that manager Connie Mack of the Philadelphia Athletics was obliged to hire a detective to guard his left-handed hurler during the latter's after-dark wanderings in search of fun. When the Rube wasn't diving off ferry boats to save imaginary drowning victims, he was wrestling live alligators to amuse a circus crowd. And yet, among all the zany activities of the great hurler, there were many genuine exploits of great heroism and bravery. Once he dashed into a burning building to save several lives. Another time, when no ambulance was available, he carried an injured teammate almost a mile to a hospital for emergency treatment. Then, to save a Kentucky town from flood danger, he stood many hours in deep water, stripped to the waist and working like a demon to help pile up sandbags against the raging waters.

It was that last incident that proved to be Rube Waddell's undoing. His harrowing ordeal during the flood resulted in serious illness. And when spring training came a month or two later, the Rube was in a hospital fighting for his own life against the tuberculosis which was swiftly destroying him.

Rube was still dreaming of joining his mates at spring training when he closed his eyes forever. The left-hander was only 37 years old at the time of his death. And there was ironic laughter even at his sad demise. For Rube Waddell, laughing and joking to the very end, passed away, as befitted a clown, on April 1, 1914.

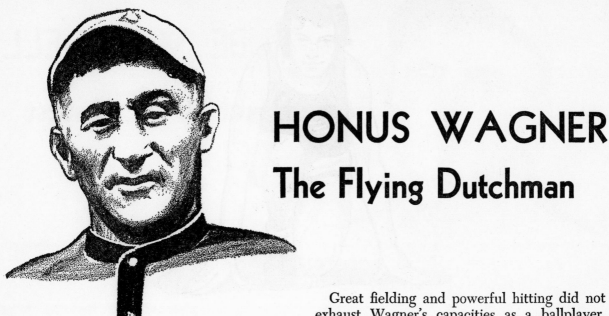

HONUS WAGNER
The Flying Dutchman

JOHN (HONUS) WAGNER was an awkward-looking broad-shouldered farm boy when he was discovered. A baseball manager idly looking from a train window saw the future great infielder throwing rocks with terrific speed and accuracy near a railroad siding. This chance encounter brought the boy his first professional baseball contract at the exceedingly modest monthly rate of $75.

Wagner was conscious of the odd appearance he presented and it made him modest to the point of shyness. But his big homely mug, the bowed legs that looked as if someone had just removed a barrel from between them, the rolling, sailor-like gait, no longer mattered when he stepped on the baseball field. Immediately he became a picture of grace and beauty. No play was impossible for him to make. Through some special magic of his own, the great Pittsburgh shortstop could grab a hard-hit ground ball that seemed sure to be out of his reach and throw out the runner without a wasted motion. Sometimes the big Dutchman did it lying down on his back. It made no difference.

At bat, Honus Wagner was the most feared right-hander of his day. Between 1900 and 1912, he led the National League in batting eight times, a tremendous record that still stands.

Great fielding and powerful hitting did not exhaust Wagner's capacities as a ballplayer. Despite his 200 pounds and his bowed legs, Honus was one of the most accomplished base stealers in the game. His total of 720 stolen bags during his career was surpassed by only three other players in history.

His versatility was no less amazing. The Flying Dutchman played at every position but catcher. And he was a topflight performer wherever he was stationed.

For 21 years Wagner roamed the Pittsburgh infield. Over that span he took part in 2,785 games, the most games played by anyone. And he made more hits than any other player in National League history, a total of 3,430. He also made the most singles, doubles and triples; batted over .300 for 17 consecutive seasons; and amassed a lifetime batting average of .329.

Devoted to the game he played so well, Honus Wagner served Pittsburgh as player and coach for 40 years. Even as an ancient gaffer well up in his seventies, the big Dutchman presented a picture of grace as he stood in the shortstop position and handled ground balls like a youngster one-quarter his age. Many came to Forbes Field in Pittsburgh just to watch him at practice before game time.

At the peak of his fame as a player, Honus Wagner was offered the then princely sum of $1,000 a week to go on the stage. The big, shy, humble guy who to many is the greatest all-around ballplayer in the history of baseball, had only one answer to make to the offer. "Sorry," he said. "I'm no actor. I'm just a ballplayer."

133

STELLA WALSH
Durable Lady

A SPORTS FAN who glances at the records made by women athletes in track and field is apt to think he is suffering from an optical illusion when he notices that in the year 1930 a girl named Stella Walsh was the United States champion at 100 yards, and that the champion at the same distance in 1948 bears the same name. But it is no optical illusion. Nor is it a different girl with the same name. The Stella Walsh who was American 100-yard champion in 1930 is the same who won the race—for the fourth time—18 years later.

A further check will show that Stella Walsh, who was Stella Walasiewicz when she came to America from Poland years ago, won many races and field events even after 1948. Her record, as brilliant as any among women in sports, includes some 70 different world and national track titles, including speed marks made nearly a quarter-century ago which have never been equaled. Outstanding among her victories was the 100-meter dash against the cream of the world's sprinters in the 1932 Olympic Games. But she has been just as outstanding in the broad jump, the discus throw and other events in track and field.

To prove that she was far from through as a topnotch performer, Stella, in 1953, entered the Western regional meet of the Women's National A.A.U. Pentathlon championship. She was well past 40 years of age. Nevertheless, Stella Walsh, competing against America's best track and field stars, spreadeagled the field. Not only did she set a new mark for the gruelling five-event contest with a grand total of 2,199 points, but she also set marks of 7.6 seconds for the 60-meter dash and 107 feet 9½ inches for hurling the discus. This was 23 years after she won her first championship!

Any woman who shattered so many records in track and field would deserve an honored place near the top of the list if she had crammed all her accomplishments into just a few seasons of competition. But more remarkable than her many triumphs is the span of years over which she met the best the world had to offer and beat them. The conclusion is inescapable. Stella Walsh is unequaled.

CORNELIUS WARMERDAM
Man On a Pole

ONE DAY, a traveling salesman, driving past a ranch in California, was forced to stop his car when his radiator began to boil over. He got out and looked around. The only human being in sight was a boy with a long pole in his hands standing in a nearby spinach patch. As the salesman started walking towards the boy with the idea of asking him where he could get some water, the young lad raised the pole and began to run. The salesman, startled, stopped in his tracks. A moment later, the young man stuck the pole into the ground, lunged forward and rose into the air. The salesman gulped. The boy was vaulting over a makeshift cross-bar. And the bar stood at well over twelve feet.

The salesman was a good friend of the track coach of Fresno State College. Once on the road, he went straight to his friend to tell of his discovery.

The Fresno State coach went back to the spinach patch with the salesman and himself watched the boy vaulting easily and gracefully over the bar. It was now up to nearly thirteen feet.

A few minutes later, the coach was talking to the boy with earnest enthusiasm. He didn't let up until he had convinced the youth to enroll at Fresno State as soon as he was ready for college. Before the coach left, he made a careful note of

the boy's name. It was Cornelius Warmerdam.

At Fresno State, coach and boy worked together as a team. The boy listened and practiced. The bar began to creep up, day by day. Warmerdam soared over at 13 feet, at 13 feet 6 inches. Soon he reached the magic 14-foot mark, one that very few men had been able to negotiate.

But the Fresno State coach had his mind set on higher things. He began to talk to Warmerdam about a pole vault of 15 feet. That incredible figure had never been attained by any living man, and no one believed it could be reached.

But Warmerdam continued to practice. Higher and higher he went. At last came the day when Cornelius Warmerdam made sports history. On the afternoon of April 12, 1940, in a track meet at Berkeley, California, the high-flying Dutchman pole-vaulted 15 feet for the first time.

To prove that the 15-foot jump was no fluke, Warmerdam did it again—and yet again. In fact, before he retired from competition, Cornelius Warmerdam reached or passed the magic figure a total of 43 times. Among those soaring flights by the young man who learned how to fly without wings in a spinach patch were both the world's indoor and outdoor records for the pole vault.

MATTHEW WEBB
The First Across

ON AUGUST 25, 1875, Captain Matthew Webb, an Englishman, became the first man in history to swim across the English Channel. He performed that then-incredible feat in 21 hours and 45 minutes. It was such a remarkable swim that thirty-six years were to pass before another swimmer crossed the 20-mile strip of treacherous water between England and France. Down through the years, many of the greatest swimmers from all the countries of the world have tried to conquer the icy cold and swift currents of the Channel—in a gamble for quick fame and fortune. Only a handful have succeeded. But most have known only bitter disappointment and tragedy!

Ironically, the fame Webb gained led him to a tragic end.

When word of his magnificent performance reached the ears of the world, a clamor went up to see this fantastic swimmer, Matthew Webb, in action. Proud of his swimming prowess, he came to the United States.

Soon after he arrived, an American swimmer named Paul Boynton challenged Webb to a long distance race to prove his claim that he was the best and hardiest swimmer in the world. To silence Boynton's jeers, Webb agreed to meet him in a twenty-five mile race. A purse of $1,000 was put up as a prize for that match race, to be held off Newport. Fortunes were wagered on the outcome.

The entire country seethed with excitement about that swimming race. On the day of the big event, Webb showed up dressed in his swimming suit. To his consternation, Boynton appeared wearing a ridiculous costume consisting of a non-sinkable pneumatic swimming suit, and he carried a pair of paddles with which he intended to propel himself. The American was more of a boat than a swimmer.

Unfair as it was, proud Matthew Webb agreed to go through with the race, for he was certain that he could outswim any rival no matter what weird contraption he wore.

The race started and for the first five miles, Webb far outdistanced his wily rival. Then after three hours in the freezing cold sea, the world's greatest and hardiest swimmer, for the first time in his life, was seized with cramps. Gamely he swam on, but before long, he began to flounder—helpless. Weeping with rage and groaning with pain, Matthew Webb was pulled out of the water. And Paul Boynton swam on for the full twenty-five miles, and claimed the victory and the thousand-dollar prize.

Matthew Webb became the laughing stock of America! Humiliated, heartbroken and depressed, the first man ever to swim the English Channel decided that he had to perform another fantastic feat to regain his shattered prestige. He would be the first man ever to swim Niagara Falls—a feat of foolhardy daring.

Certain that he would regain his honor, the gallant Englishman, leaped into the dangerous Niagara rapids and started to swim—in a mad effort to vindicate himself. It was his last bid for fame. He drowned!

The Human Fish

JOHNNY WEISSMULLER

AS A BOY, Johnny Weissmuller was frail and sickly. The doctors gloomily shook their heads over him. One physician, however, had an idea. He suggested that the youngster try swimming exercises to build up his strength.

"But I hate water!" protested Johnny.

"A boy of 13 ought to love to swim," said the doctor.

"But I can't swim a stroke!" said Johnny. "I've never tried it in my life."

Johnny's father verified what the boy said, and added that neither he nor Mrs. Weissmuller could swim either. The doctor again looked at the puny boy. "Try it," he said finally. "I think it'll do you good."

A very reluctant Johnny made his way to the muddy Des Plaines River near his home. Hating every minute of it, the boy started paddling around in the shallow water near the bank. He was clumsy and awkward, and he would have quit after his first attempt but his parents made him continue with his exercises.

Gradually, as Johnny learned to swim he learned to enjoy the water and as his fun increased, his ability grew faster and his strength grew with it. Later, when he moved close to Lake Michigan, he saw for the first time really skillful swimmers. He was now interested enough to observe them closely. Soon he was imitating various swimming strokes. And, as time passed, the other swimmers began to watch Johnny. For this once sickly weakling had become a first-rate swimmer. He didn't stop there; he became a great one, one of the best in all the world.

All in all, Weissmuller set the astounding total of 67 swimming records. When the Olympic games of 1924 came along, Johnny was on America's swimming squad—and from that athletic carnival he emerged as the world's greatest swimming star.

Again, in 1928, Johnny led the American swimming team into the Olympics—and again he came out as the greatest of swimming champions.

All the world acclaimed Johnny Weissmuller. The name became a standard for swimming greatness. In the years that followed his triumphant accomplishments, no swimmer ever rose to prominence without being compared to him. And to this day the same comparison is made. Still the saying is heard: "He may be good, but he is no Johnny Weissmuller."

It has been a long time since the boy who took up swimming because he was so frail became America's incomparable swimming champion. Yet, when the experts gathered to choose the greatest swimmer of the 20th century, one name led all the rest—the name of Johnny Weissmuller!

The Splendid Splinter
TED WILLIAMS

HE WAS as cocky and brash a rookie as ever reported to a major league training camp. No one ever displayed more confidence in his own ability to hit the ball. When the training camp broke up, the rookie learned that he was to go back to the minors for another season. Before he left, he had a word or two to say to the veteran outfielders who were sticking with the club.

"I'll be back," he said. "And before I'm through, I'll be making more money than all you guys put together."

That was 19-year-old Ted Williams talking, and no man ever made a boastful remark with more truth in it. The following year, as a freshman in the majors, Ted batted .327. And he went on from there.

In his second season, Ted hit .344 and established himself solidly as one of the most fascinating figures in the game. Tremendous as was his clouting, his prowess at the plate was overshadowed by other things. He bickered and

quarreled constantly with players, public and press. He was loved by some, hated by many. His childish fits of temper alienated him from players and fans alike. He refused to acknowledge the cheers of the crowd and seemed to have little regard for his teammates or for team play.

The high spot in his batting life came in the season of 1941, his third with Boston. Ted came down to the last day of the season with an average for the campaign of .401. No one had posted a .400 mark in some twenty years. The Red Sox were scheduled to play a double-header with the Philadelphia Athletics on that final day. Williams could have stayed on the bench and preserved his stratospheric batting mark, since neither team was going anywhere and it made little difference whether Boston lost or won. But Ted insisted on playing out the string. "I don't want to win anything sitting on the bench," he growled. "If I can't hit today like I have all season then I don't deserve to own a .400 average."

So Ted played in both games. He made five hits, boosting his already swollen average to .406.

In 1943, the Marines grabbed Williams and sent him off to war. He lost three seasons of major league play. In '46 he was back with the Red Sox. For the first time, Ted showed his remarkable capacity for making a comeback. In the four years that followed his return from the war, he hit .342, .343, .369 and .342.

The old pro was playing in the All-Star game in 1950 when he slammed into the outfield wall during the first inning and shattered his elbow. He told no one of his injury and played into the ninth inning while suffering intense pain. After that, he did not play for a long time. But he came back, as he had before, to play again— and through his hitting to reach the salary figure of $100,000 a year as baseball's biggest star.

Again in 1952, the Marines sent out a hurry call for Ted Williams. He was 34 then, but off he went to Korea to fly jets. He flew 39 missions, miraculously escaping death several times. Finally he was sent home, worn, battered and tired.

Ted had had little hope of returning to baseball the day he left for Korea. But he got himself back into shape as best he could in time to play the last 37 games of the 1953 season. And what a comeback that was! In 91 trips to the plate, he made 37 hits, including 13 home runs. His average for that tail-end of 1953 was a clinking .407!

When the 1954 season started, Ted was back for another try. The 36-year-old star was only 18 minutes in spring training camp when he fell chasing a fly and broke his shoulder. This time it was certain that old Ted Williams was through for good. How could an old veteran like Williams come back from a smashed shoulder to play again?

Two-and-a-half months after the accident, Ted returned to the Boston Red Sox. A lot of hardware that held his shoulder together had been removed except for one last steel pin. Every time he moved his arm, the shoulder hurt like blazes. But Ted went into the line-up for a double-header his first day back. And, in the most dramatic comeback any player ever made,

he went to bat 9 times and slammed out 8 hits— five singles, a double and two home runs!

That was Ted Williams, the comeback kid. Every time he was knocked down by adversity or fate, he returned with even more muscles in his bat to prove to the remaining doubters, if any, that he was still the greatest hitter alive. Meanwhile, the dislike that had so long been leveled at him, was beginning to fade. Other stories about the great slugger came out into the open. It was learned that he had given a clubhouse boy his entire end of a World Series cut plus some $500 out of his own pocket. It became known that Ted spent many hours in the hospitals cheering up sick kids. Without fanfare, he was taking other kids out fishing and paying all their expenses. And it was noted that he had stopped popping off at fans and newspaper men.

A lot of people changed their minds about Ted Williams. But like him or not, there's one thing no one can get away from. Ted Williams is baseball's greatest slugger of his time. And the figures are there to prove it.

HELEN WILLS

Little Poker Face

THE GIRL WHO WAS one day to become Queen of the Nets and the outstanding competitor among women in tennis began to play the game as a child because her only playmate, a boy, wanted to play tennis and nothing else. Helen Wills did not care for the game at first. But her father, who played moderately well, patiently taught his little daughter how to play, and he proved a good teacher. When, on her 14th birthday, she managed to beat him for the first time, Doctor Wills presented her with a membership in the Berkeley Tennis Club as a reward.

At the club, little Helen saw for the first time what real tennis looked like. She was able to meet on the courts some really good players. Among the club players was the immortal champion Billy Johnston, and it was his mighty forehand drive that inspired Helen Wills to lash out at the ball in imitation of the international star. So thrilled was she by the power of her own first hard drive that she continued to practice power-stroking until, at last, she became the hardest hitter among women.

The girl of 14 with her two long braids was soon playing with such skill that she won the Pacific Coast Junior championship. She went on the following year to capture the National Junior crown at Forest Hills. It was then that her apparent calmness and absence of facial expression won her the nickname of "Little Poker Face." When she was just 17, in 1923, she defeated the great Molla Mallory in the finals to win her first United States Women's National tennis championship.

Thus began the most glorious championship saga in tennis history. She followed up with a win at Wimbledon, classic event in the world of tennis. In 1926, she played her only match against the incomparable Suzanne Lenglen with the whole world hanging on the result. Lenglen won and the two never met again. The great French star faded rapidly from public attention but Helen went on to greater glory. She won at Forest Hills again and at Wimbledon, won the French title, and repeated the victories over and over again.

All in all, Helen Wills won the two most

coveted titles—the United States Nationals and the Wimbledon singles—more times than any other woman in history. The U. S. crown fell to her 7 times; the English one, 8 times.

In 1933, Helen Wills lost her American title to Helen Jacobs in a match that Miss Poker Face was not able to finish because of a back injury. As she limped from the court, the crowd jeered the dethroned champion. Two years later, after a series of treatments to her back, Helen Wills returned to tennis. Like the great champion she

was, she made a dramatic comeback at Wimbledon. There, in the singles finals, she defeated the girl who had toppled her from the championship heights two years before in one of the most thrilling matches ever seen at that historic place.

Then Helen Wills left tennis, never to play again. But the world will always honor "Little Poker Face" as the woman tennis champion who won more world titles than any other woman in history.

GAR WOOD

OF ALL the motorboat drivers in history, Gar Wood is foremost. In his racing days he was practically unbeatable. Some of the records he set stood for over a quarter of a century, notably his 70 miles per hour in the Gold Cup competition of 1920, and the 1932 Harmsworth Trophy mark when he drove his famous Miss America X at the incredible speed of 124.86 land miles per hour.

It was in 1920 that Wood made his first notable contribution to motorboat racing history. England had been holding the Harmsworth Trophy, symbol of world supremacy, since 1913. Wood and his Miss America I wrested the trophy from England. He never lost it for America thereafter, defending successfully eight times against England's best drivers, who spent more than $7,000,000 to build and race boats against him in the vain attempt to win it back.

From boyhood, speed was the passion of Gar Wood. Gar's father was a steamboat captain who ran a clumsy old tub on Lake Osakis in Minnesota. At that time, there was a rival boat on the lake competing with Gar's father. The two captains developed a feud that became more and more bitter as the years passed. One day, they decided to settle their differences by racing down the lake. The winner would gain the coveted right to enter the harbor first.

Gar took his place on deck with his father as the race began. The two lumbering vessels moved down the lake side by side, belching heavy clouds of black smoke. After a short time, Captain Wood pushed his straining boat into a short lead and held on grimly. Then, with only half a mile to go, his boat ran out of fuel for the furnace. The vessel began to lose way and the race seemed surely lost.

It was then that young Gar gave the first indication that he would some day become the most determined boat racer in history. While his father stood by fuming and bewailing his bad luck, young Gar went into action. Grabbing an axe, he began to chop furiously at the furniture on the boat. "Come on, dad, and help me!" he shouted as he swung. "This furniture will make fine fuel. You don't want to lose this race, do you?"

Captain Wood hesitated a moment, then pitched in to help his son. In a few minutes they had smashed enough furniture into wood for the furnace to get blazing again. The Wood boat began to creep ahead once more. At the finish line they were well ahead, the winner!

That was how Gar Wood started his speed boating career. He built and raced many great boats. Money for them came from the fortune he amassed inventing important machines, particularly a hydraulic hoist. But while his inventions brought him wealth, it was motorboat racing that brought him fame. His domination of one of the most dangerous sports in the world assures him of a high place in American sporting history.

CY YOUNG
The Cyclone

A BIG, HUSKY FARM BOY living at a place called Gilmore, Ohio, in 1890 heard rumors that fellows were being paid good money by professional clubs to play baseball. The youngster made his way to Canton and looked up the manager of the local club.

"I'd like a tryout," said the boy.

The manager inspected the tall figure before him. "What do you do?" he asked.

"I can throw 'em a little," answered the farm boy.

"Go ahead and throw," said the Canton manager.

The boy took the mound just as he was, in street clothes. The Canton manager sent his star slugger to the plate. The boy in the pitcher's box waited.

"What are you standing there for?" barked the Canton manager. "Start throwing!"

"Don't I get a catcher?" asked the boy.

"What for?" sneered the Canton pilot. "Think you'll get one past the batter? Aim at the back fence."

So the boy started throwing. Pitch after pitch whistled past the bewildered slugger and slammed with terrific force against the wooden fence. Not once could the batter connect, not even to tick it for a foul.

The Canton manager looked at the fence in amazement. It had been smashed to splinters. "Looks like a cyclone hit it," he said. "If you keep throwing them like that, they'll be calling *you* cyclone!"

"You going to hire me?" asked the boy.

"Guess so. How much do you want?"

"Better talk to my dad," said the boy. "Here he is."

The Canton manager turned to the boy's father. "How much for your boy?" he asked.

"Well," drawled the boy's father. "He's a mighty fine pitcher. Reckon he ought to be worth all of $30 a month to you."

"It's a deal," said the manager quickly. "What's your name, boy?"

"Young," said the farm boy. "Denton True Young." And then he smiled bashfully. "But you can call me Cyclone if you want to."

Cyclone was soon shortened to Cy. And before the 1890 season was over, he was sold to Cleveland for, it was said, a suit of clothes. His salary rose to the giddy height of $1,400 a year. And one of baseball's greatest stars was on his way to glory.

Before he was through, Cy Young had set a flock of records in baseball. No one pitched as many years as he, in as many games, or won more. Over a space of 22 long years, he worked in both major leagues. He pitched in 906 games, winning 511 of them. He struck out 2,819 batters and won between 20 and 36 games annually for 14 years. He hurled three no-hitters, one in the National, two in the American League. The no-hitter he pitched for Boston against the Philadelphia Athletics in 1904 was a perfect game, no opposing batter reaching base. In that same year, he pitched 23 consecutive hitless innings, also a record.

Once, on the eve of an important series, Cy was approached by certain unsavory characters. He was offered $20,000 to let up in his pitching and let the opposing team beat him. The offer must have been a tempting one to a man getting only $4,000 a year. But the big pitcher did not hesitate. He took the hoodlums by the back of the necks and flung them out of his hotel room. And he went on to win every game he pitched in the series.

Young was the first hurler to be elected to Baseball's Hall of Fame. With all the changes that have taken place in the game since he made his fantastic records, it is highly unlikely that his feat of winning 511 games can ever be equaled. Oddly enough, the record might have been even greater than it was. For Cy Young could still pitch winning ball when he left the game. He was nearly 45 when he called it a day, and the hop was still on his fast ball. Unfortunately, the passing years had put a lot of surplus weight on his big frame. And when he found he had grown too fat to field bunts, Cy Young hung up his glove in disgust with himself.

But he didn't leave in disgrace. His last effort on the mound, for the Boston Braves in 1911, was against the Philadelphia club which started a rookie half his age. The rookie, himself to become a Hall of Famer under the name of Grover Cleveland Alexander, beat him 1–0 in a brilliant pitching duel. It was a fitting close to the career of baseball's winningest pitcher!

EMIL ZATOPEK
Incredible Czech

WHEN EMIL ZATOPEK, a soldier in the ranks of the Czechoslovakian army, first entered an official track meet, the experts stared at him with startled disbelief.

"Look at him!" exclaimed one track judge, "He runs like a man who's been stabbed in the heart!"

Zatopek was that unusual sports figure, a self-taught runner. As a soldier, he had spent all his spare time awkwardly running up and down the rugged hills of his country, while burdened with heavy hobnailed boots and with his soldier's pack on his back. His fellow-soldiers were sure he was crazy. But Zatopek, the rugged peasant, never stopped, for he was running to catch a dream. His dream was to make himself into the world's greatest runner, so that he could escape from obscurity into a happier life of fame.

Thus, without form and without training, Zatopek ran and ran, punishing his 165-pound body with clumsy and tireless foot racing. Finally he caught the dream. He became a hero of the 1948 Olympic Games, and a superman of the same event in 1952. He emerged from that international sports meet with three championships and three world's records! For the first time, one man had swept all three of the most gruelling Olympic distance classics—the 5,000-meter run, the 10,000-meter, and the marathon race.

By the end of 1953, the man they had mocked as "that crazy soldier" had shown himself to be the greatest distance runner of all time. For Emil Zatopek, the incredible formless madman with the ugly, straining running style that was no style at all had set eight world records! At 31, he held world's records for the 10,000, 20,000, and 30,000 meters, also for the six-, ten- and fifteen-mile races, as well as for the one-hour run. No other man in history ever held eight world records in running at the same time!

World fame as a distance runner brought Emil Zatopek the rewards he had run to catch. His Czech army mates no longer taunted him with shouts of: "Soldier, stop running! You're crazy!" They now cheered him and saluted him as an officer with the rank of major. In Czechoslovakia, Zatopek became a national hero.